CRITICAL THINKING IN
YOUNG CHILDREN

CRITICAL THINKING IN YOUNG CHILDREN

Jane Davis-Seaver

Mellen Studies in Education
Volume 50

The Edwin Mellen Press
Lewiston•Queenston•Lampeter

Library of Congress Cataloging-in-Publication Data

Davis-Seaver, Jane.
  Critical thinking in young children / Jane Davis-Seaver.
    p. cm. -- (Mellen studies in education ; v. 50)
  Includes bibliographical references and index.
  ISBN 0-7734-7749-7
  1. Cognition in children. I. Title. II. Series.

 BF723.C5 D37 2000
 155.4'1342--dc21   00-032453

> This is volume 50 in the continuing series
> Mellen Studies in Education
> Volume 50 ISBN 0-7734-7749-7
> MSE Series ISBN 0-88946-935-0

A CIP catalog record for this book is available from the British Library.

The Edwin Mellen Press   The Edwin Mellen Press
Box 450   Box 67
Lewiston, New York   Queenston, Ontario
USA 14092-0450   CANADA L0S 1L0

The Edwin Mellen Press, Ltd.
Lampeter, Ceredigion, Wales
UNITED KINGDOM SA48 8LT

Printed in the United States of America

to Les, Kerry, Cameron, Larry, Scottie, Chip,
Brittany, Aleksey, Kaitlyn and Dillan

TABLE OF CONTENTS

i

PREFACE

Educational innovations come in many guises. The two most prevalent types are programmed and mutually adaptive innovations. Programmed innovations are not initiated in a response to a significantly felt need to change among school staffs but from perceived needs of the policy makers. Innovations such as these specify in detail a set of behaviors that users must demonstrate before the innovation is considered fully implemented. They ignore the specifics of institutional contexts and are based upon some particular group's definition of what the goals and means of what educational change should encompass. Examples of programmed innovations include those in which the innovation is fixed and unchangeable. These include as teacher-proof curriculum packages and computer assisted programs that stress basic skills. Despite the good intentions of their originators, programmed innovations often become just another set of educational recipe books with which the non-reflective teacher can lay upon his or her lap. In short, anyone can do it and thus programmed innovations are destined to gather dust in the cloakroom when the next new and improved model comes down the educational pike.

Mutually adaptive innovations suggest that educational change can be accomplished only through learning by doing when they are accompanied by a commitment to solving problems. They focus on the conceptual development of the user rather than upon the development of the treatment. They cannot be reductionistically prepackaged in advance. Instead, mutually adaptive innovations evolve over time and can be modified depending upon the needs and problems of specific contexts. They demand that the curriculum be developed locally, that planning and that further education be continuous.

Jane Davis-Seaver's text, *Critical Thinking in Young Children*, is an example of a mutually adaptive innovation. Davis-Seaver suggests that young children, are quite capable of thinking deeply and critically about the problems which erupt within their lived experiences and that this level of thinking need not cease when children walk through the classroom door.

But adopting and implementing Davis-Seaver's ideas will not be easy nor hurried primarily because teachers who adopt the worldview that education need not be a straight-line business must first come to grips with a number of other ideas. First, they must recognize that they will need to climb down from their high horses and allow the messiness of learning to hold sway. Once teachers decide to give children their heads, the learning environment will no longer be ordered but the dynamic of chaos will fuel the learning of their students. In addition, as children freely employ their higher order thinking skills, they may delve into a myriad of topics that may challenge the status quo. They may, as Bertrand Russell suggested in his essay *On Education,* begin to wonder why some people live poverty and why others make war. Thirdly, this text is not for the educationally faint-hearted but for those "radical wannabe teachers." When critical thinking becomes the core of instructional planning, teachers must acknowledge that they will need to become well acquainted with the literature of critical thinking. They will need to read the writings of Frank Smith, Henry Giroux, Howard Gardner, John Dewey, Michael Apple, and Maxine Greene. They will not be spending their planning periods in the teacher's lounge poring over those instructional magazines searching for arts and crafts ideas. They will become more intellectually astute and because of this, will run the risk of distancing themselves from those of their colleagues who prefer to sit in the stands and watch the game from afar. Finally, the teacher who picks up this text and can't seem to put it down, who begins to peer through the keyhole onto another world must realize that the ideas posited here will not be the only way to separate the embers of the real from the fires of the artificial. Rather it is only the beginning of a lifelong journey.

Thomas J. Smith, Ph.D.

North Carolina A&T State University

ACKNOWLEDGMENTS

Many people helped immeasurably with the production and completion of this book. Expert advice from Dr. D. Michelle Irwin, Dr. Svi Shapiro, Dr. Kathleen Casey, Dr. Fritz Mengert, and Dr. Jan Williamson is greatly appreciated. The children who were the participants in the research were charming, forthright and eager to share their thoughts with me and they have made a major contribution to the understanding of what children think about their thinking and how they go about doing it. A special thanks goes to my granddaughter, Brittany, who was not only an active participant in the research but a prime supporter in helping me get it completed. A place in heaven is surely reserved for my husband, Les, who was supportive and encouraging throughout the process and who patiently straightened out all the computer glitches and mess-ups that I created while writing this. Thanks also go to my colleagues in public school, Ed Allred, Betty Brown and Mary Kay Forbes, and at N.C. A&T State University, Dr. Tom Smith and Dr. Dorothy Leflore, who have encouraged and advised me.

1

CHAPTER ONE

CRITICAL THINKING AS EDUCATION

From the point of view of the constructivist teacher who sees education and its attendant curriculum goals as the result of children learning through resolving cognitive conflicts through experiences, reflection and metacognition, critical thinking is at the heart of the teaching and learning process. Such education has as its purpose the fostering of a way of looking at events, experiences, assumptions and conclusions such that the status quo is challenged, alternate and creative solutions to problems are considered, and communication, whether written or spoken is clear, reasonable, meaningful and thoughtful. It assumes that all children can think in depth, albeit some more than others, and that it is such thinking that brings about meaningful learning of basic concepts that are applicable and transferable. It further assumes that experiences, direct rather than vicarious, are vital to the critical thinking process and that, for young children, only through such experiences and the struggle with discrepancies, oddities and anomalies does understanding occur. Such a teacher bases the curriculum and instruction in the classroom around this premise and uses many creative solutions to the diverse ways of learning that children bring to the schooling situation. This presupposes a thoughtful analysis of not only how concepts are uncovered by the child, but also of the physical, emotional and cognitive environment of the classroom itself.

The basic concepts of critical thinking are several. Being able to understand or figure out what the problem (or conflict, contradiction) is and to direct thinking to the specific purpose of solving the problem, understanding the frames of reference or the points of view involved are important. Identifying and understanding the underlying assumptions, basic concepts and ideas involved as well as understanding the theories and principles that are being used are also basic. Critical thinking also includes citing evidence, data and reasons and their interpretations, following lines of thought that are advanced, and understanding inferences, implications and consequences. (Paul, 1990; Beyer, 1985; Nosich, 1993). There is a creative component to strong critical thinking such that originality, freshness and inventiveness are brought into the problem-solving and applications.

This being so, the constructivist teacher sees critical thinking as the process of interacting within the materials and data of a discipline in such a way as to come to a deeper understanding of the basic ideas that drive the theories of the discipline, that create new concepts both within and transferred to other disciplines and make relevant to one's own life the concepts of that discipline. It is critical thinking then, that makes radical (Giroux, 1992) education a way of life rather than a set of facts to be memorized, retold, and then forgotten after fulfilling a certain prescribed set of steps over a prescribed length of time.

Critical thinking applications to education and curriculum are commonly found in middle and high school. They are seldom included at primary and elementary levels, and those few attempts to do so are reductionist in nature. (Lipman, 1988; Ennis, 1994; Paul, 1990) The question at issue, then, is whether this process can begin in early childhood classrooms, and how it can begin in such a way as to make critical thinking a life-long tool for managing change and diversity.

In recalling my earliest awareness of my own thinking, I can remember that I did my best thinking when I was messing about with materials that I was interested in. I have always liked animals, and I learned more about them from finding them in the wild (i.e. snakes and bugs) or looking after them at my grandmother's farm or having them as pets at home. In remembering school, I recall doing some very creative things with art materials, only to have the teacher tell me that I hadn't followed the directions. Once in art class, we were given construction paper and told to make a farm scene on a sheet of light blue paper. Everyone else cut out animals, colored them, and pasted them onto the paper. The teacher stapled all the papers to the bulletin board until she came to mine. "*This* won't go on the board," she said as she threw it into the trashcan. "Next time look at what everyone else is doing and do it that way." My error was to have made a three-dimensional scene so that the paper needed to sit on top of a table instead of flat on a bulletin board. I even made the cow's heads so they would bob up and down when you pulled their tails, but since it didn't fit the teacher's idea of what she wanted, into the trash it went. Was this critical thinking? For a young child, it is a very important part of critical thinking: that of finding an alternative way of doing something or looking at materials that generates a creative way of solving a problem, in this case that of producing a farm scene from construction paper.

Later, as a teacher of young students and as a student of critical thinking theory, I could see that young children seemed to be doing a lot of critical thinking, of problem-solving in creative and imaginative ways, of finding new ways of looking at situations. As I observed their learning and thinking, I found that they could do some very sophisticated thinking about the experiences that they had. And I observed that such thinking occurred along with the experiences, not afterwards, and did not occur in lieu of the experiences. In addition, it seemed to me that it was the interaction, the discussion of their perceptions that generated the understanding rather than any teaching of skills on my part.

I sensed a conflict between what I was reading about children's thinking and what I remembered about my own thinking and what I was observing in the young children I taught. For example, one of the foremost promoters of higher order thinking in young children and a proponent of the skills-driven approach to critical thinking, Matthew Lipman, wrote that

It is just too much to ask of students that they acquire at one and the same time the skills that a subject presupposes, which students must bring with them, and the skills needing to be learned in order to think in the subject. (Lipman, p. 31)

He recommends instead that

...the teachers at any grade level teach their students the skills that will be needed in subsequent grades, not the skills needed at their own grade level, for those skills will have been implanted in the students earlier on...(Lipman, p. 31)

and then concludes "*That children should behave philosophically should be sufficient.*" (italics mine.) (Lipman, p. 179)

What he seems to be inferring is that by being able to perform such skills as, for example, constructing sentences of the if/then format and using them in prescribed instances such as are found in his books for children, the child is behaving philosophically and therefore, once all the skills of philosophic behavior are acquired, the child is then able to think critically about philosophical issues.

Although Lipman recommends philosophy as a way of teaching children to think, a view with which I can agree, when he designed a series of books to do this, he did so from a male, Eurocentric and elitist point of view that is unfit for the classrooms of today. For example, he says "We all know that philosophy emerged in Greece about a hundred generations ago..." (Lipman, 1988, p. 11). And his books, he explains, are peopled with characters he designed to be models of learning behavior for the children who read them (p. 6) and contain stories intended to become "a paradigm for the live children in the classroom" (p. 6). As I read this, I thought about my Native American students, my Asian students, my African-American students, my Indian, Jewish, and Arabian students. All of them come from cultures with highly developed philosophical thought as old or older than Greek philosophical thought. And I wondered what kind of critical thinking this could be? And would this kind of thinking, that of holding up one kind of philosophical thinking as correct or best, foster true critical thinking among my students?

This view seemed to be in line with behaviorist thinking that posits that the behavior defines the learning. That is, if a student can produce an appropriate behavior, then the thinking will follow the behavior, and that behavior is evidence of internalization of the skill and can now be transferred to new situations. For example: If, when shown a picture of three ducks and a chicken, the young child can mark the chicken as the one that doesn't belong, then this approach assumes that the child is developing an understanding of the concept of categories. Or, in the case of Lipman's series, if the students can construct a series of if/then type sentences they now understand the logic of philosophy. This is a way of shaping thought with the outcome controlled by the teacher, not a way of teaching a skill to be used by the child to produce an outcome under her own control and direction.

I began to wonder if perhaps teachers, even well-intentioned ones, are doing young children a disservice by not giving them opportunities to use higher order thinking even though many knowledgeable people seem to imply that they can't do it, or that they can only do so much in very specific ways. Elkind (1988), for example, echoes Piaget in discussing stages of thinking in children:

> ...although children think, it is not until adolescence and the appearance of formal operations that young people think about thinking...Thinking about their own and other people's thinking is a unique achievement of adolescent mental operations. (Elkind, p. 112)

Taking into consideration the implications of Piaget's formal reasoning stage appearing in adolescence, and Erikson's psychosoical crisis of industry versus inferiority in early school years, the Hunter (six-step) method of teaching led teachers to concentrate on transmission of facts and to leave reasoning and critical thinking to a later time.

I also was aware of the conflict in critical thinking theory between the skills-oriented perspective (Ennis, 1994; Lipman, 1988, Ruggiero, 1991) and the more holistic and content-dependent approach (Parks and Swartz, 1992; Paul, 1990; Weil, 1992). Because these ideas drive curriculum and instruction, and the controversy between the rational, Eurocentric and the political, transformative philosophers has implications in the diverse classrooms of early childhood, they serve as the basis for my research into critical thinking in early childhood education.

My approach to this research

Frank Smith, (1986) in disagreeing with a programmatic, step-by-step approach to skills acquisition in learning to think critically says

...thinking in critical ways involves far more than learning a set of skills. Such a reductionist attitude could only interfere with the development and expression of critical thought, by focusing on extraneous "training" aspects and ignoring essential situational, individual, social - and political - factors. (Smith, p. 105)

He says also that in order for children to think critically, they must have the authority to do so, and that it must matter to them to do so. He explains

One reason that critical thinking is broken down into numerous components is to make it fit into the constraining framework of current testing and instructional technology. Did the designers of such packages themselves become thinkers by learning to select the odd man out, the geometrical design that does not belong, or the best way to ferry missionaries and cannibals across a river? Could such considerations ever authorize anyone to think critically? The expectation that students and teachers should follow rigid guide lines of exercises, tests and discrimination might be seen as the antithesis of fostering critical thought. (Smith, p. 106)

He continues

Children learn to think critically when they have opportunities and reason to think in critical ways; when they see (or hear) others engaged in critical thinking; and when they are admitted into arguments, challenges and debates based on respect rather than power or exploitation. (Smith, p. 107)

Duckworth (1987) also endorses the idea that thinking critically about something important to the student is the best way for children to learn to think critically. She says

Teaching linguistic formulas is not likely to lead to clear logical thinking; it is by thinking that people get better at thinking. If the logic is there, a person will be able to find words adequate to represent it. If it is not there, having the words will not help...Drilling children in sentences of the "if/then" format is not likely to develop in them the notion of logical implication...there is no need to give children "language tools" in order to facilitate clear thinking, intelligence, or greater knowledge. (Duckworth, p. 25-7)

And so, because this line of thinking about children's thinking, coincides more closely with my observations of children and my own experiences, it is from this latter perspective that I address this research. I believe that children can indeed think critically about matters of concern to them, matters that are an integral part of their lived experiences. I believe that they learn to think critically by thinking critically; that is, the process of critical thinking is endemic to the outcome of becoming a critical thinker. I believe that teachers must empower children to think critically through the structure of the classroom and the methods that they use in facilitating the learning and thinking that takes place there.

As a researcher, I found that in order to become a party to the thinking of young children, I had to leave behind my preconceived notions about what they should be thinking or how they should be thinking. I had to listen and encourage, and challenge them with material from their every day life. Then, they would let me join them in their world, so I could see them make meaning of their experiences from their own very unique perspective. I asked them to engage in metacognition to find out about their thinking at a time when they had very little formal experience in doing so. In order to discover this metacognitive behavior, I needed to listen to what these children were saying without evaluating it from an adult point of view. After reading much of the literature on what adults had to say about how and what young children think, I wanted to find out what young children themselves had to say about their own thinking, and how I might apply this knowledge in the early childhood classroom.

Definition of Terms

Abstract thinking: In the Platonic sense, that thinking which is pure thought unconnected to concrete reality; in the Piagetian sense, formal reasoning or logico-mathematical thinking which is characterized by the ability to express thoughts through the manipulation of symbols without any representation of concrete reality.

Constructivist: A teacher who facilitates learning by affording students the opportunities to construct their own knowledge and theories through interaction with materials, ideas and experiences that stimulate their own thinking; a philosophy that advocates such teaching. This philosophy says that understanding comes about through the child's struggle with the data rather than memorization of it; that motivation comes from the relevance of the problem to the child's own life; that the classroom is child-directed; that the child is an active participant in the learning process rather than a passive recipient.

Creative thinking: That thinking which is characterized by originality and novelty; diverse thinking. It is that part of critical thinking that poses an original, fresh and inventive approach, solution or application to a critical thinking process or outcome.

Critical thinking: Purposeful thinking that uses the skills of problem solving, decision making, evaluation, and metacognition to resolve conflicts, arrive at solutions and understand in depth. It is that part of the creative thinking process that analyzes and evaluates the appropriateness and logicalness of the creative process or outcome.

Developmental: Having to do with growth over time, a patterned sequence of change.

Metacognition: Thinking about one's own thinking as one is thinking.

Programmatic: Having to do with a program; for example, a program of instruction such as a teacher's manual, or prescribed steps toward a goal; an imposed strategy.

Reductionist: Having to do with the philosophy that learning can be reduced to small bits of knowledge which can be taught in isolation and then put together again; teaching that progresses from part to whole, that reduces skills to their smallest components to be learned.

11

CHAPTER TWO

TALKING TO THE CHILDREN

A qualitative approach is the most appropriate and realistic for exploring children's spontaneous thinking. Qualitative research is marked by its subjective, narrative nature. Mishler (1990) says that

> ...a hallmark of interpretive research..is understanding how individuals interpret events and experiences, rather than assessing whether or not their interpretations correspond to or mirror the researcher's interpretive construct of "objective" reality. (Mishler,p. 427)

Such research is likely to be made up of a series of interviews with a small number of persons, sometimes only one, and the analysis will consist of looking for patterns, trends, categories of response and relationships. The conclusions of the researcher grow out of the data after it is obtained, and it sometimes changes when subsequent interviews are conducted. It may not be replicated even though the same question may be asked of other interviewees, because the analysis as well as the response to the questions are interpretative. The same data, then, can possibly be interpreted in alternative ways subject to the perspective of the researcher. Peshkin (1988) says

12

...I decided that subjectivity can be seen as virtuous, for it is the basis of
researchers' making a distinctive contribution, one that results from the
unique configuration of their personal qualities joined to the data they
have collected. (Peshkin, p. 18)

Patti Lather (1990) writes that

No longer does following the correct method guarantee true results,
rather, "method does not give truth; it corrects guesses"...Whereas
positivism insists that only one truth exists, Rich (1979) argues: "There is
no 'the truth' [nor] 'a truth' -- truth is not one thing, or even a system. It is
an increasing complexity" ...[qualitative research] allows a search for
different possibilities of making sense of human life, for other ways of
knowing which do justice to the complexity, tenuity and indeterminacy of
most of human experience. (Lather, p. 259)

Language and Form

The language of qualitative research is one of dialogue, of participants, of
praxis and transformation. Results are often presented in narrative, or story
format, and the researcher and participant together construct the knowledge that
the research brings out. It was important to the information I wanted to search on
an equal basis with the children into their thinking, to analyze it as it came about
rather than from my ideas as to what it should be. The effects of such a search for
meaning would be transformative for both researcher and participant, and one that
we would experience together.

My original intention was to ask one question, to which the students could
reply in any way they wanted. This did not work. In reply to the question "Tell

me about your thinking?" I got a lot of blank tape, some "um's" and much fidgeting. It turned out that a conversation format was much better. I would pose the questions, "What do you think thinking is?" and "Tell me about a time when you did some thinking?" then follow the child's lead until another nudge was needed and off we'd go again. The "nudges" consisted of such comments as "Are you saying ..." or "are you telling me that ..." and "you said earlier ..." Occasionally I might ask for an example or a comparison, and often I simply repeated what the child said in different words for clarification.

Because of the constraints of time --the ten children had only a limited amount of time out of their class or at my home --and the realities of being six and seven years old, I held most of my conversations with the children down to twenty minutes or less. Usually, they let me know when they were through talking, and they were very pleased to come back each time. I spent at least forty-five minutes in a series of three sessions with each student; three of the girls and one of the boys spent an hour with me in four sessions.

Validity

To some researchers, qualitative research lacks validity because it does not respond to mathematical formulas, nor can it be easily replicated. (Glass, 1984). It is interpretive and subjective in nature, and the "biases" of both researcher and participant are in full view of the reader. For the statistician, these are seen as weaknesses, (Glass, 1984) but Mishler (1990) writes, "Clearly, this form of inquiry-guided or "grounded theory" research...involves a continual dialectic between data, analysis, and theory. Its steps are no more mysterious or less attentive to the data than statistical procedures." (Mishler, p. 427) He continues

The discovery -- of the contextually grounded, experience-based, socially constructed nature of scientific knowledge -- should be cause for celebration rather than despair. It does not dispense with methods for systematic study but locates them in the world of practice rather than in the abstract spaces of Venn diagrams or Latin Squares. (Mishler, p. 436)

The validity of this paper, then lies in the actual experience and uniqueness of the method rather than depending on replication. What is true about these children's thinking is "true" because they have told me so. And because common threads run through the thinking of all of them, I have learned something about children's thinking in general that I can use in the classroom.

Their ideas about what good thinking and bad thinking are, and their consequences, are important aspects of this research. Other threads such as common definitions and applications of thinking, common logic and strategies, as well as their understanding of the politics of thinking have influenced my conclusions.

Research Participants

I decided to interview ten six- and seven-year-old children who were not identified as exceptional in any way, either "gifted" or "handicapped" -- just regular kids. I thought that ten children would be a manageable number as well as varied enough for me to look at differences as well as finding patterns and trends in their thinking.

I did not want exceptional children for two reasons. The percentage of children in special classes at either end of the spectrum is small, and they are being taught in non-standard ways. So often in the studies that I have looked at, psychologists have tested and experimented with exceptional children and then extrapolated their results to the entire population. This does not seem reasonable to me. To base instructional strategies for ninety percent of the school population on the ten percent who have learning difficulties or who need highly individualized instruction seems to me to be in error.

After consulting with a first grade teacher, I arranged for her to send three of her students to me to talk about my research and see if they wanted to participate. She chose two boys and a girl who readily agreed to talk with me. The three chosen were good students who occasionally made the honor roll and generally kept up with their classwork and homework, at least enough to be out of the room for a while with me. Two were six years old, and one was nearly seven. Two were in their second year of school, and one was in the third year having been enrolled in a Pre-K classroom. The other seven students, selected by this and other teachers, I saw either at their home or at my home. They were, like the first three, six and seven years old, had been in school at least two years. There were three boys and four girls, and all were considered good, but not exceptional, students. I interviewed all the children one at a time, using an audio tape recorder and transcribing the interviews later myself.

CHAPTER THREE

PERSPECTIVES ON CRITICAL THINKING

Historically, there are three general perceptions of critical thinking, perhaps as a result of differences in the definitions of thinking and its relationship to definitions of critical thinking. One perception arises from a reductionist conception of thinking in which critical thinking is often broken down into skills, dispositions, or attitudes. Another perspective arises from the developmental concerns of Piaget and Erikson, and thus delegates much of critical thinking to post-adolescent schooling. A third stance comes from constructivism which says that critical thinking develops not through maturation or through practice and repetition of skills in artificial situations, but through thinking critically in situations that are meaningful to children of whatever age.

The Reductionist Viewpoint

The reductionist is concerned with individual skills that have been identified as behaviors that critical thinkers engage in, and therefore the mastery of these skills which can be taught directly will result in critical thinking. Some reductionists (Adams and Hamm, 1992) feel that the foundation for critical thinking begins with accumulating enough facts or knowledge such that the child will have something concrete to think about. Others (Ennis, 1994; Lipman, 1988;

Ruggiero, 1991) attack the problem from the other side, that of teaching thinking skills first and then integrating them into content.

The specific skills vary according to categorization but not to definition. Dispositions, for example, are comparable to affective strategies; abilities to cognitive skills. Ennis (1994) defines critical thinking in terms of three basic dispositions: caring to get it right, (seeking alternatives, endorsing a position to the extent that it is justified, and being well informed); representing a position honestly (being clear, determining focus, offering reasons, accounting for the total situation, seeking precision, awareness of basic beliefs, seriously considering other viewpoints); and caring about the dignity and worth of every person (listening to others' viewpoints and reasons, avoiding intimidation and confusion, and concern for others' welfare.) He also lists fifteen abilities of the critical thinker which he groups into those which involve clarification, metacognitive abilities, and auxiliary critical thinking abilities (not constitutive of being a critical thinker.)

Paul (1990) offers a list of skills of critical thinking which he breaks down into strategies labeled affective strategies, cognitive strategies - macro-abilities, and cognitive strategies - micro-skills. He has also developed a chart in which he compares the perfections of thought with imperfections of thought.   Lipman (1974), in Harry Stottlemeier's Discovery seems to reduce philosophy to an exercise in logic, and later (1988) says of this teaching method "That children should behave philosophically should be sufficient." (p.179)   In a resource publication for the Institute for Critical Thinking, (1988) he explains that

> Critical thinking, as we know, is skillful thinking, and skills are proficient performances that satisfy relevant criteria...the mobilization and perfection of the cognitive skills that go to make up critical thinking cannot neglect any of these skills without jeopardizing the process as a

whole. This is why we cannot be content to give students practice in a handful of cognitive skills while neglecting all the others that are needed for the competency in inquiry, in language and in thought that is the hallmark of proficient critical thinkers. (Lipman, p. 11)

It is not in the theory as much as in its application that we experience the full implications of such reductionist ideas. Ruggiero (1991) says that thinking is any mental activity that is directed toward problem-solving, decision-making or understanding with both creative and critical dimensions, and he advises balancing practice of discrete skills with holistic exercises requiring the use of both critical and creative processes. However, he likens critical thinking skills to other kinds of skills in that "Like other skills, thinking must be practiced regularly in a variety of situations to be maintained." (1991, p. 2) This is reminiscent of the training aspect of some learning theories. And in his Lessonpack for Creative and Critical Thinking (1990), a pre-packaged program with an identified sequence of skills, for teachers to use in their classrooms, he advertises a single lessonpack which "will serve all your teachers and students", which is "brief", and which "enables all teachers to distribute the same explanatory handouts, thus creating continuity and reinforcing learning." Swartz (1990) calls attention to its "separable modules that can be inserted in any number of places in a standard high school or college course", some teachers cite its usefulness as "homework assignments", and Paul (1990) advocates its use for teachers "who want to foster critical and creative thinking in their students but have not yet had time to study the underlying theory." Ruggiero (1990) himself advertises that

Unfortunately, few teachers have been trained to teach thinking, and those that have often lack the time to develop effective classroom materials. LESSONPACK solves this problem by providing both

> explanatory handouts and challenging assignments for students. The
> handouts are so clear and comprehensive that even untrained teachers can
> approach thinking instruction confidently. (Ruggiero, p.4)

Obviously, to this way of thinking about critical thinking instruction, it is not necessary for the teacher to understand critical thinking. She is merely the instrument through which the skills are transmitted, and modeling the kind of thinking desired is not a component. The idea that critical thinking, with its components of dialogue and cooperative reflection, can be done in solitude as homework strains credulity.

This idea that teachers do not need to be a vital part of the curriculum, but merely transmitters of it is addressed by Michael Apple. He writes, "Whether we like it or not, the curriculum in most American achools is not defined by courses of study or suggested programs, but by one particular artifact, the standardized, grade-level-specific text..." (Apple, p. 24) And, he explains, these books are not just books that the children read and use, they are also economic commodities. He says, "While the text dominates curricula at the elementary, secondary, and even college levels, very little critical attention has been paid to the idealogical, political, and economic sources of its production, distribution, and reception." (Apple, p. 24) The problem, as he sees, it is one of power and empowerment based on economics rather than sound educational or pedagogical practices. The bottom line is profit, and research and testing is promoted that pushes the use of the book or kit in order to raise the test scores.

One example of a reductionist curriculum is the Improving Social-Awareness-Social Problem Solving (ISA-SPS) Project at Rutgers University and University of Medicine and Dentistry of New Jersey-Community Mental Health Center (UMDNJ-CMCHC) at Piscataway (cited by Elias, 1992) which developed a curriculum-based approach to critical thinking in elementary grades. He explains:

In what is called the Instructional Phase, students receive focused instruction in social decision making and problem solving. They are taught an eight-step strategy that is presented in a cumulative manner and grouped into 44 topic areas (22 presented in an initial year and 22 in a subsequent year). The ISA-SPS teachers chose a format that emphasizes the learning of a discrete skill that will be linked to others for maximal retention and use...field testing indicated the need to emphasize review and practice...Video tapes are used at the upper elementary level to provide, for example, more sophisticated stimuli for observation, recall, modeling, guided practice and discussion. It also allows for a cohesive instructional sequence of at least two years, with two levels of material to be mastered. (Elias, p. 12)

The links to learning theory are clearly implied in Reed and Polumbo's 1992 of BASIC, a study of computer instruction aimed at improving problem-solving skills in other areas of the curriculum:

Designing a curriculum to enhance a problem-solving approach would first introduce students to simple, isolated commands and then later to the chunking of commands...Such an approach would include, at different stages, the provision of "prompts" or sample ways for solving specific programming problems, these prompts would be extremely rigid at first and then, as the treatment progresses, would fade (or become less rigid), allowing for the students to make more decisions about potential solutions...(Reed, pp. 313-4)

They found that this did not increase problem-solving skills in other areas until after a significantly long period of time of practice had occurred, and only when it was measured by instruments that specifically measured the skills taught. They surmised that studies, which implied that studying BASIC as a transferrable skill is contraindicated, were flawed because they used instruments that did not correspond directly to what was being taught.

It is the reductionists' theory (Adams and Hamm, 1992) that until a number of facts or an accumulation of data can be acquired, critical thinking cannot take place. It is not the age of the child, nor is it the maturational level, that determines when critical thinking begins. It is, instead, the amount of knowledge that has been accumulated that determines when critical thinking can begin. Thus, in this line of reasoning, although a person may be maturationally able to reason formally, if there is no data-bank, as it were, of knowledge to call on, then critical thinking must be delayed.

The Developmental Perspective

The developmental perspective, however, says that the ability to think critically depends upon physical/biological maturation (Piaget, 1972) or upon the successful resolving of psychosocial tasks at a maturational level (Erikson, 1963). Vygotsky (1934) looks at the developmental aspects of the formation of concepts, concepts being for him higher-order thinking, and concludes:

The development of the processes that eventually result in concept formation begins in earliest childhood, but the intellectual functions that in a specific combination form the psychological basis of the process of concept formation ripen, take shape, and develop only at puberty. Before that age, we find certain intellectual formations that perform functions similar to those of the genuine concepts to come. With regard to their composition, structure, and operation, these functional equivalents of concepts stand in the same relation to true concepts as the embryo to the fully formed organism. To equate the two is to ignore the lengthy developmental process between the earliest and the final stages. (Vygotsky, p. 106)

He explains that this development comes about because of the development of verbal ability. Thus, for Vygotsky, while critical thinking is present in undeveloped form in early childhood, its mature form can be seen only as the child matures into adulthood. He also implies that a young child that is given no opportunity to think critically while young, will not develop into a critical thinker in adulthood. He continues the analogy:

No new *elementary* function, essentially different from those already present, appears at this age, but all existing functions are incorporated into a new structure, form a new syntheses, become parts of a new complex whole; the laws governing this whole also determine the destiny of each individual part. (Vygotsky, p. 108)

For Vygotsky, then, the maturing of thinking like the maturing of the body, does not develop any new parts, any more arms and legs, for instance, but those parts that are already there become different in maturity and in proportion, and are used in affectively different ways.

Piaget (1972) says that the child restructures thinking at each stage through the process of assimilation and accommodation and that this thinking is conceptually different at each stage. It is the interaction with the physical and social environment that is the motivator for the movement to another stage of development. He divided the cognitive development of the child into three major stages which he describes as

...The period of sensorimotor intelligence. This first period extends from birth to the appearance of language, that is, approximately the first two years of existence. (Piaget, 1972, p. 54.)...The period of preparation and of organization of concrete operations of categories, relations, and numbers. We will call concrete operations those we bear on manipulable objects (effective or immediately imaginable manipulations) in contrast to operations bearing on propositions or simple verbal statements (logic of propositions). This period extending from about two to eleven or twelve years can be divided into a subperiod A of functional preparations of the operations but of preoperatory structure, and a subperiod B of operatory structuration itself . (Piaget, 1972, p. 56)...The period of formal operations....Above all what appears in this last level is the logic of propositions, the capacity to study statements and propositions and no longer only objects placed on the table or immediately represented. (Piaget, 1972, p. 60)

Because the child has neither the cognitive structures in place nor the experiences necessary for formal reasoning until adolescence, according to Piaget, he would advise the teacher of the young child to provide experiences that would predispose such reasoning rather than formal reasoning itself.

Problems with Piaget for the critical thinking theorists who would like to see critical thinking begin in early childhood arise from the notion that abstract thinking or formal reasoning is the same as critical thinking. In contrast to abstract or formal reasoning which Piaget defines as manipulation of symbols without connection to concrete objects, critical thinking has to do with how thinking is done and not necessarily with what. As I will show in my analysis of childrens' thinking, it is possible for a young child to think critically long before thinking symbolically, that is formally or abstractly. Such criteria as reasoning

25

from an alternate viewpoint, examining evidence and basing predictions or decisions on evidence, making reasoned judgements, and solving problems creatively within a dialogical and dialectical format do not require the ability to reason formally. I will cite many examples of such thinking among the six- and seven-year-old children that I interviewed.

Dewey (1910) sees thinking as developmental but not necessarily with regard to age. He explains that thinking develops by progressing from the concrete to the abstract. He defines concrete as "...a meaning definitely marked off from other meanings so that it is readily apprehended by itself." (Dewey, p. 136) He explains:

> The meanings of some terms and things, however, are grasped only by first calling to mind more familiar things and then tracing out connections between them and what we do not understand. Roughly speaking, the former kind of meanings is concrete; the latter abstract...The difference as noted is purely relative to the intellectual progress of an individual; what is abstract at one period of growth is concrete at another; or even the contrary, as one finds that things supposed to be thoroughly familiar involve strange factors and unsolved problems...*These limits are fixed mainly by the demands of practical life.* (Dewey, p. 136-7)

He says that these practical demands are such as taxes, elections, wages, the law, and so on, things that are a part of our adult everyday life and thus are concrete to the adult. To a child, however, such things are not part of everyday life, and therefore abstract. He does not see the hierarchy that the reductionist sees. He explains that he does not consider theoretical thinking higher than practical thinking. He writes, "A person who has at command both types of thinking is of a higher order than he who possesses only one." (Dewey, p. 142)

Dan Weil, (1992) a developmental and critical thinking theorist, discusses readiness for reasoning. He explains:

I have unfortunately heard too often from colleagues and administrators alike that primary school children simply aren't developmentally ready for critical thinking activities, that we need to concentrate first on teaching them skills: the skill of reading, the skill of writing, and the skill of decoding. They'll have plenty of opportunities to think later, the argument goes. Besides, many argue, kindergarten should be simply a place where children learn to play. A place where they learn the skills of cut and paste and play together. We couldn't disagree more. (Weil, p. 13)

He explains that although skills such as reading, writing, and decoding are important in early childhood classrooms, that teaching them does not preclude teaching thinking at the same time, and that neither kind of skills should be taught in isolation. He points out:

Certainly the appropriateness of instruction is crucial to successful learning. For this reason we argue that in shaping critical thinking activities for children in the early ages, we must recognize their developmental readiness. But to abandon reasoning about conflicts and problems in the early grades in favor of trivial pursuits and a skill-intensive curriculum, arguing that students will learn to think later is to do a disservice not only to today's elementary students, but to society in general. (Weil, p. 13)

He goes a step further by saying that not only is critical thinking developmentally appropriate, but it is a developmental necessity.

Parks and Swartz (1992) recommend infusion across the curriculum and at all grade levels as a technique to combine appropriate subject content with critical thinking skills. Theirs is not a pre-packaged program of detailed lesson plans, but an explicit method that teachers must adapt to the developmental needs and academic levels within their classrooms. Parks explains, "The thinking instruction we offer is direct in the sense that it is very explicit and well organized." (p. 2) Swartz says, "...for deep understanding to occur, content really has to be taught in ways that help students make use of decision making, problem solving, and judgment." (p. 2) They feel that infusion is effective because as it combines the instruction of content with the instruction of thinking skills, students understand the content more fully because of the thinking involved. They explain that grade designation for certain thinking skills presents a false view of the way thinking occurs, that a certain skill can be learned at fourth grade but not in second, for example. They say that it is the instructional method that must adjusted developmentally, not the type of thinking.

The Constructivist Perspective

While Weinstein (1991) says that "...the critical thinking movement has not yet consolidated around particular pedagogical models, nor carefully addressed the relationship of critical thinking to other educational ideals, for example, mastery of content and cultural transmission" (Weinstein, p 18), it seems that the constructivist model most nearly resembles the instructional model embraced in theory by critical thinkers. The fit between constructivist methods of struggle with and reflection upon experiences and data, and the critical thinking methods of dialogue, questioning and reflection is one that facilitates both critical thinking and construction of knowledge.

Paul (1990) recommends a dialogical model, with risk-taking and struggle at its core. He says, "There is no way to take the thinking out of knowledge, or the struggle out of the thinking, just as there is no way to create a neat and tidy step-by-step path to knowledge that all minds can mindlessly follow." (p. xv) However, he then, in true reductionist manner, breaks down the thinking into neat and tidy steps which he recommends for everyone. On the other hand, Brooks and Brooks (1993) explain:

A constructivist framework challenges teachers to create environments in which they and their students are encouraged to think and explore. This is a formidable challenge. But to do otherwise is to perpetuate the ever-present behavioral approach to teaching and learning. (Brooks, p. 30)

They explain that such teaching begins with a problem that is relevant to the child, either directly or through teacher mediation, and then gives the student time to pose, challenge and answer questions that arise out of the problem and possible solutions. Such an approach sees critical thinking not as an add-on but as an integral part of the curriculum.

Such problem posing and questioning methods that lead to empowerment as well as thoughtfulness are themes that Maxine Green (1991) considers. She writes:

Wide-awakeness, situatedness, intersubjectivity, reflexiveness, constructed knowledge, achieved meanings: these have been some of my themes as I have struggled to move from a treatment of thoughtfulness to a view of legitimate critique...We are charged, we who care about thinking and teaching, to study that equation (addiction to harmony and fear of contradiction) and keep trying to discover what does not "add up."

We may be able to find connections that enable us to do something about the desire to suberge in a comfortable life, the tendency to believe blindly, the dedication to profit, even the self-infatuation of the few. (Green, p. 21)

For Greene, as for Giroux (1993), critical thinking takes on political as well as introspective connotations, and like Duckworth (1987), the struggle to discover what doesn't "add up" is implicit in her definition of critical thinking.

For many, the constructivist perspective encompasses critical thinking as the major component of a comprehensive definition of education itself. In fact, Morgan (1993) defines education in terms of both constructivism and elements of critical thinking theory He says:

Education is not in the "business" of providing human resources to industry and commerce. Education implies a seeking to understand, the preparedness to approach difficult problems -- problems of significance to human beings. Education in today's changing world means becoming the architect of one's own meaning; participating fully in the great conversations of our culture, and being able to ascertain the significance of their meaning. Education means not just thinking critically and creatively, but doing both well. (Morgan, p. 15)

Gardner (1993) agrees with this perspective, and explains:

...I would say that many schools and educators do not even have the idea that understanding is both important and elusive. Most schools are bent upon the mastery of facts, even though facts have nothing to do with disciplinary mastery or with understanding. Most standardized tests are also fixated on the accretion of facts. Thus, everything from our teachers to our tests to our television game shows projects precisely the wrong image of what it is to be an educated person. (Gardner, p. 3-4)

The Constructivist Teacher

Duckworth (1987) in explaining her idea of the constructivist classroom, says that in order for young children to think critically, they must be given time and opportunity to do so. The constructivist teacher, she says, must not only be open to young children's ideas and accepting of them, but also must provide a setting that enables them to be caught up in ideas of their own making. She feels that when children are given the opportunities to be intellectually creative their general intellectual ability is enhanced. Her concept of struggle in order to understand is like Dewey's (1910) idea of thinking as a way of being in the world, of being alive. Wonder, excitement, curiosity, puzzlement, and what she calls "dawning certainty" (p. 67) are part of the real struggle to make meaning and come to an understanding of real problems and their solutions. Knowing the right answer, she explains, is the most passive of intellectual functions and is one she considers automatic and thoughtless.

The constructivist approach to learning and thinking begins with where the students are at the time, and with what they already know. Morgan (1993) says, "We have linked education with schooling. For us, this is a linkage of convenience rather than one of reality, for most of what we know is not learned in school." (p. 17) Barell (1991) also addresses this. He writes,

One of our challenges then, is to create settings where students' thinking is encouraged as a natural process in school. As one student said, "I think outside school. Here [in school] I memorize stuff." We can change this perception and help students become more thoughtful as they are learning school subjects. (Barell, p. xiii)

He recommends that in order for students to think well in schools, we as teachers must give them not only opportunities to do so but also the authority to do so. He writes:

It is, therefore, necessary to emphasize from the very first day of school that this is *our classroom:* Here we work together toward common goals. Here everybody has some responsibility for his/her learning and for that of others as well. Students will not and cannot feel empowered if everything is done for and to them. If they have no opportunity to set goals, design strategies, and feel responsible for these decisions, they will leave school with less than a feeling of confidence in their own ability to take control of their own lives. (Barell, pp. 70-1)

He explains that children come to school with many questions, with the potential for posing questions that will form their challenge to us and the rest of the world. Schools, he says, and adults do more to stifle thinking and question-posing than any other element, and he thinks this is because of accountability to state and local assessments, to covering content and other such restrictions. To give children opportunities to explore, to question and to take risks is to create a rich environment for critical thinking.

The Critical Thinking Perspective

Everyone grounds their work in a particular perspective. I find the critical thinking perspective offers the most productive arena for me to look at the question of how young children think about their thinking. There are many definitions of critical thinking. I have limited my review to just two -- the works of Richard Paul and Henry Giroux. They represent two rather different aspects of the various issues within the critical thinking field: Paul, the rational and reasonable critical thinker; and Giroux, the passionate and political critical thinker.

A comparison of their definitions of critical thinking and the implications for the classroom shows that while they agree on many important points, they diverge on many others. A consideration of both points of view gives a broad view of critical thinking both for today's students and for tomorrow's citizens.

Giroux's Definition of Critical Thinking

Giroux addresses first a comprehensive definition of critical thinking, and then formulates three principles that he says are guides for critical thinkers to act upon. He writes

At the level of understanding, critical thinking represents the ability to step beyond commonsense assumptions and to be able to evaluate them in terms of their genesis, development, and purpose. In short, critical thinking cannot be viewed simply as a form of progressive reasoning; it must be seen as a fundamental political act. In this perspective, critical thinking becomes a mode of reasoning that, as Merleau-Ponty points out, represents the realization that "I am able" meaning that one can use individual capacities and collective possibilities "to go beyond the created structures in order to create others." (Giroux, 1981, p. 57)

Giroux's three principles of critical thinking are that of negativism, contradiction, and mediation. Because, he says, "dialectical critique begins with a rejection of the `official' representation of reality," (Giroux, 1983, p. 64) the principle of negativism

...refers to a thorough questioning of all universals, an interrogation of those "received" truths and social practices that go unquestioned in schools...represents a mode of critical engagement with the dominant culture, the purpose of which is to see through its ideological justifications and explode its reifications and myths. (Giroux, 1983, p. 64)

The principle of contradiction

...is informed by the assumption that the contradictory nature of social reality in the wider sense, and school life in particular, invalidates mainstream appeals to the imperatives of social harmony and the logic of consensus. (Giroux, 1983, p. 64)

The principle of mediation, he writes, is

...a form of refusal, a proving of those aspects of school life that appear to "speak" for themselves, that are presented in such a way that they can be judged only in their immediacy...(and)...points to the need for a theory of critique that focuses on the nature and construction of thought itself. It examines self-critically how thought is constructed and produced, and looks at both its intentional and unintentional consequences...it provides the groundwork for reappropriating and restructuring those aspects of dominant and subordinate cultures that enhance the possibilities for critique and self-determination. (Giroux, 1983, p. 65)

Thus, for Giroux, a critical thinker is one who questions knowledge that is presented as *a priori*, or self-evident, looks for the assumptions on which knowledge is based, considers implications and alternative outcomes and solutions, and works for a restructuring of those parts of school life that do not support and facilitate critical thinking. Giroux equates critical thinking with political action, and says that critical thinking as a pedagogical tool "models a form of resistance and oppositional pedagogy" (Giroux, 1983, p. 62). He asks teachers to "place notions of critique and conflict at the center of their pedagogical models." (Giroux, 1983, p. 62)

Schools using Giroux's ideas of critical thinking would not be filled with quiet classrooms with students working individually at their seats on worksheets providing drill and practice on isolated skills. Instead, he says

First the active nature of students' participation in the learning process must be stressed...students are able to challenge, engage and question the form and substance of the learning process. (Knowledge) must be seen as a critical engagement designed to distinguish between essence and appearance, truth and falsity...Second, students must be taught to think critically. They must learn how to move beyond literal interpretations and fragmented modes of reasoning...learn to juxtapose different world views against the truth claims that each of them makes. Facts, concepts, issues and ideas must be seen within the network of connections that give them meaning. Students must learn to look at the world holistically in order to understand the interconnections of the parts to each other...to speak with their own voices, to authenticate their own experiences...become aware of the dignity of their own perceptions and histories...and begin to examine the truth value of their meanings and perceptions, particularly as they relate to the dominant rationality. (Giroux, 1983, p. 202)

Thus, for Giroux, the dialogical and dialectical nature of the classroom combined with a classroom pedagogy that encourages questioning, challenging, and looking at issues from many perspectives built on the active, hands-on construction of knowledge by the students themselves is one where our society restructures its future to a more democratic society.

Paul's Definition of Critical Thinking

Richard Paul says that

Humans are the only animal whose thinking can be characterized in terms like clear, precise, accurate, relevant, consistent, profound, and fair; they are also the only animal whose thinking is often imprecise, vague, inaccurate, irrelevant, superficial, trivial and biased. Critical thinking makes sense in light of this paradoxical dichotomy. Humans shouldn't simply trust their instincts. (Paul, p. 44)

In his handbook as well as in his other writings, Paul also deals with three aspects of critical thinking as he calls the perfections of thought, the elements of thought, and the domains of thought. He cautions that although there is critical thought which is sophistic and used only for the betterment of the vested interests of the thinker, the critical thinking which he is concerned with teaching to children is "fairminded critical thought" which he describes as that which "meets epistemological demands regardless...is characterized by empathy and devotion to truth...is consistent in the application of standards." (Paul, p. 32) He defines fair-minded critical thinking as

> ...disciplined, self-directed thinking which exemplifies the perfections of thinking appropriate to a particular mode or domain of thinking...is disciplined to take into account the interests of diverse persons or groups... (Paul, p. 33)

Paul then gives a list of the perfections and imperfections of thought. Perfections, as he sees them, are "clarity, precision, specificity, accuracy, relevance, consistence, logicalness, depth, completeness, significance, fairness, and adequacy for purpose." (Paul, p. 33) The imperfections are the opposites of those qualities of thought, namely, "unclarity, imprecision, vagueness, inaccuracy, irrelevance, inconsistency, illogicalness, superficiality, incompleteness, triviality, bias or one-sidedness, and inadequacy." (Paul, p. 33) He concludes, pessimistically, however, that "There is no society yet in existence that in a general way cultivates fairness of thought in its citizens." (Paul, p. 34).

Next, Paul gives a listing of the elements of thought:

> These include an understanding of and an ability to formulate, analyze and assess: 1) the problem or question at issue; 2) the purpose or goal of the thinking; 3) the frame of reference or points of view involved; 4) assumptions made; 5) central concepts and ideas involved; 6) principles or theories used; 7) evidence, data or reasons advanced; 8) interpretations and claims made; 9) inferences, reasoning and lines of formulated thought; and 10) implications and consequences which follow (Paul, p. 52)

It is important for students to understand and be able to use these elements of thought, Paul says, because, "Focusing on the nature and the interrelationships of the elements of thought illuminates the logic of any particular instance of reasoning or of any domain of knowledge." (Paul, p. 53)

Looking at the domains of thought, Paul explains that the critical thinker must adjust such thinking to the frame of reference, the social situation or the established logic of the issue in question. He recommends using a multilogical approach even when the issue is monological in order to help students consider many alternatives. (Paul, pp. 35-36)

Further refining his definition of and explanation of critical thinking, Paul looks at the traits of mind of the critical thinker. He says

Consider intellectual humility. To become aware of the limits of our knowledge we need the courage to face our own prejudices and ignorance. To discover our own prejudices, we must empathize with and reason within points of view we are hostile toward. To do so, we must typically persevere over a period of time, for reasoning within a point of view against which we are biased is difficult. We will not make that effort unless we have the faith in reason to believe we will not be deceived by whatever is false or misleading in the opposing viewpoint and an intellectual sense of justice. We must recognize an intellectual responsibility to be fair to views we oppose. We must feel obliged to hear them in their strongest form to ensure that we are not condemning them out of ignorance or bias on our part. At this point we come full circle back to where we began: the need for intellectual humility. (Paul, p. 54)

Thus, for Paul the critical thinker is one who reasons logically, fairly, and rationally, with humility, continuing until a reasoned judgement can be made on the issue by the thinker who will at the same time admit that other equally logical and rational judgements can also be made by another. He says, "...critical thinking is best understood as a global way of disciplining and taking control of one's own thinking so as to accomplish more effectively the purposes of thinking through disciplined self-command. (Paul, p. 397)

Implications of Critical Thinking

While Paul sees the importance and urgency for teaching critical thinking, Giroux expresses his concern in more political language. In fact, Giroux considers critical thinking a political act, and for school children, the necessary beginning of many political acts to come. He sees the lack of critical thinking in the schools as a direct result of the positivist philosophy of education growing out of the industrial sector of the economy of the United States. And he blames educational researchers for not opposing, or worse yet supporting, this philosophical bent. He charges researchers with bowing to the pressures of the dominant functionalist ideology and the conservative principles of social harmony and normative consensus. (Giroux,1981, p. 5).

Paul agrees with this, and echoes Giroux's sense of the acute nature of the problem when he writes

Only if we raise children to think critically, as a matter of course, about their use of language, the information they take in, the nature of propaganda which surrounds them, the multiple prejudices assumed to be self-evident truths; only if we educate children to probe the logical structure of thought, to test proposed knowledge against experience, to scrutinize experience from alternative perspectives; only if we reward those who think for themselves, who display intellectual courage, humility and faith in reason; only then do we have a fighting chance that children will eventually become free and morally responsible adults and hence help eventually to create, through their example and commitments, genuinely free and moral societies. (Paul, p. xviii)

Both philosophers agree that critical thinking holds the key to the continuance of democracy and an open society. While Paul says critical thinking is foundational to a genuine democracy, Giroux says that it is required in order to reconstruct the conditions necessary for a radical change to true citizenship.

Theories of Knowledge

Paul and Giroux base their theories of critical thinking on their assumptions about knowledge and how it becomes known. In discussing his proposal for a radical educational theory, Giroux says that knowledge "must be seen as a historical and social construct..." (1981, p. 81) and further says that, "Cognition, in this sense, is not simply contemplation, it is the understanding of reality insofar as humankind shapes it in the process of living it." (Giroux, 1981, p. 115)

Paul says that "We need to remember that all knowledge exists through critical thought" (Paul, p. 47) and that it "must be understood as the consequence of a perfecting discipline of thought, of learning to think critically." (Paul, p. 50) He continues, "When knowledge is separated from thinking and presented as a thing in itself, it ceases to be knowledge." (Paul, p. 154)

For both Paul and Giroux knowledge is equated with an understanding of reality and can only come about through thinking which is both social and political. For both philosophers, this view of knowledge is essential to their view of what is needed for understanding, but for Paul thinking seems to lead to a mutual understanding of knowledge, whereas for Giroux knowledge is more a matter of understanding and negotiating the differences in reality among persons than in coming to any consensus about it.

Changes in Educational Philosophy Needed

Both Richard Paul and Henry Giroux see global implications in the need for critical thinking and an educational philosophy that incorporates it as one of its major tenets. Paul writes

A multidimensional, interdependent world cannot be fathomed by people schooled in fragmented, monological specialties or steeped in nationalistic myopia. Most problems are multidimensional, logically messy, require interdisciplinary analysis and synthesis, deeply involve values and priorities, and demand sympathetic consideration of conflicting points of view or frames of reference. (Paul, p. 19)

Giroux would like to see changes in educational philosophy to reflect more closely the issues of struggle to enhance the quality of life for the general public and aim more forcefully toward a more radical view of democracy He explains, "Democracy is a celebration of difference, the politics of difference, I call it, and the dominant philosophies fear this." (Giroux, 1992, p. 11)

Giroux, in a much stronger sense than for Paul, sees critical thinking meaning the betterment of the individual which for him means that "social betterment must be the necessary consequence of individual flourishing." (Giroux, 1992, p. 11) Paul is concerned with the betterment of the individual and realizes that eventually this will bring about the betterment of society. However Giroux feels that when an individual gains a better understanding of reality, truth, knowledge through critical thinking, it is imperative that this individual take active steps to use that understanding for the benefit of others and to bring about a more genuinely democratic society.

A reading of Paul's writing does not generate either the urgency that one finds in Giroux's work, nor the pessimism about the present state of critical thinking. While both acknowledge that there is not enough of it going on, Giroux says, "It does not seem unreasonable to conclude at this point that critical thinking as a mode of reasoning appears to be in eclipse in both the wider society and the sphere of public school education." (Giroux, 1981, p. 57) And he lays the blame for this state of affairs directly at the feet of positivism and its practitioners who, he feels, adulate facts and empirically obtained knowledge without an understanding of its contingent nature, thus grounding critical thinking in "the politics of `what is'". (Giroux, 1981, p. 51)

A Radical Pedagogy for Schools

Both Giroux and Paul advocate beginning with the schools to make changes in how the larger society views its ability to deal with reality. Both see value in dialogical and dialectical thinking and find that unless students become accustomed to such thinking that they are ill prepared for life outside school. Paul says, "Divergent and conflicting points of view are essential. Schooling without this carefully cultivated diversity cannot be educational. It cannot lead to fairmindedness, objectivity or comprehensiveness of view." (Paul, p. 16) Giroux, on the other hand, while just as concerned that children learn to think critically in order to solve problems, sees the problem with not thinking critically as one of lack of empowerment which he defines as "the ability to think and act critically." (Giroux, 1992, p. 11) This is different from Paul's rational, measured critical thinking. Giroux sees such empowerment as, "...providing students with the opportunity to develop the critical capacity to challenge and transform existing social and political forms, rather than simply adapt to them." (Giroux, 1983, p. 47) He defines radical education as one that questions received assumptions and institutions and the bases of all disciplines toward the aim of making all of society more democratic for everyone. (Giroux, 1992, p. 10) He says that schools must use what he calls a radical or border pedagogy in order to accomplish their mission of teaching students to think critically. He dismisses the idea that the main purpose of public education is economic efficiency, and says further that education must go beyond critique to encompass the language of empowerment and possibility. (Giroux, 1992, p. 10).

Border pedagogy, he says

respects the notion of difference as part of a common struggle to extend the quality of public life...also links the notions of schooling and the broader category of education to a more substantive struggle for a radical democratic society. (Giroux, 1992, p. 28)

Giroux makes explicit his idea that to think critically, one must act critically, which for him is a political act. Paul addresses this same notion, although not in a political sense as he recommends

...the Socratic philosophical tradition reflected in the Critical Thinking movement. This approach emphasizes cultivating a certain sort of person, the "rational person," conceived of as whole and integrated and as involving affective as well as cognitive dimensions. (Paul, p. 172)

He sees this approach as important to the individual student in order to think through events and problems that occur in everyday life in order to heighten the quality of life individually. He feels that this is the first step to an eventual increase in the quality of life in a democratic society, but there are no elements of the radical, and political, tone as in Giroux.

However, Paul does not picture the critical thinking student as one without passion. This is necessary for the development of the rational person, he says. He calls for a curriculum based on the Socratic philosophical tradition and using dialogical and dialectical exchanges as a way of learning. He explains, "All or most of what we learn rationally requires dialogical exchanges and opportunities to judge between conflicting points of view." (Paul, p. 212) He says that such a curriculum cannot be programmatic in nature and must be expressed in broad outlines. He explains

...the largest and most important form of human thinking, dialectical thinking, cannot, by its very nature, be reduced to an "operational procedure." When we think dialectically, we are guided by principles not procedure, and the application of the principles is often subject to discussion or debate. (Paul, p. 96)

Conclusions

Richard Paul and Henry Giroux share many ideas about critical thinking. They are in general agreement that critical thinking is a rational consideration of many perspectives, that clarity of language is important in expressing the thinking to others, it involves both dialogical and dialectical interaction with others, it is fairminded, and addresses the issues at hand within the logical framework of the domain. They also agree on what traits the critical thinker possesses. Such traits as intellectual humility, perseverance and the ability to speak with their own voices are valued by both. The search for the truth in the face of appearances is considered most important in both philosophies.

Both Giroux and Paul feel strongly that schools are the best places for critical thinking experiences to begin, and both imply that unless school children are allowed these experiences they will not be able to survive well in a dialogical and dialectical society at large. They call for a classroom of challenges, questions and opposition, and recognize critical thinking as the source of any real knowledge obtained by the students. And both see critical thinking as a holistic activity, one that, while it can be domain specific, cannot be fragmented into subject matter if it is to be effective.

The major difference between the philosophy of the two men lies in the implications they hold for the act of critical thinking. On the one hand, Paul sees critical thinking as necessary in order for human beings to make reasoned judgements about everyday issues. He sees these acts as ones that will make life better, more understandable, and more under the control of the thinker. Because of this, life will, in general, eventually become better for everyone. He sees critical thinking as empowerment for the individual to take control of the everyday events of everyday life, to rationally set goals and reach them, and to make reasoned and logical inferences about the issues at hand.

Giroux, however, sees critical thinking as a political act that empowers the individual to become a challenger of "business as usual" society, to question the assumptions and truth claims of the dominant ideology and to move forcefully to remake society into a more democratic world for the betterment of everyone, even those who do not think critically themselves.

Although Paul speaks of a passion for intellectual, logical, ethical reasoning, he does not speak with the same passion that Giroux does. Paul's passion is an individual passion that seeks personal truth while also ensuring that others are also free to seek their individual personal truths for which the thinker has empathy and respect. Giroux's passion is a collective one, one that demands that individuals think critically individually in order to act critically collectively for the betterment of society and those that come after.

My concern with these definitions of critical thinking is with their application to young children and the place critical thinking plays in the early childhood classroom. If critical thinking is the basis for genuine democracy and radical citizenship, and I do think that it is, what can I as an early childhood educator do with young children that will make this a viable basis for curriculum and teaching in early childhood classrooms?

CHAPTER FOUR

CAN YOUNG CHILDREN THINK CRITICALLY?

The purpose of this study is to examine what young children have to say about their thinking in order to determine if they are thinking critically about issues which concern them whether in school or out of school. The hypothesis of this study posits that young children can think critically in school if opportunities are given them to do so, and that they are already thinking critically outside of school because even at the early ages of six and seven their world requires them to do so. That there is a relationship between the necessity for thinking critically and the ability to do so is also shown in this analysis.

The method used in this study is dialogue between the researcher, the participants and the literature of reductionist, developmental, constructivist and critical thinking theory. Although the two specific critical thinking theorists cited in depth, Paul and Giroux, represent dialectical viewpoints on critical thinking, their combined criteria are applied to the interviews to determine critical thinking on the part of the children. Central themes and issues that grow out of the children's conversations are used to determine the intertextuality of the children's critical thinking and the critical thinking criteria of Paul and Giroux.

Basic themes and issues that are addressed in this chapter are definitions of thinking, strategies for decision-making and problem-solving, reciprocity, metacognition, thinking in school vs. thinking outside of school, adult manipulation of children's thinking, validating truth claims, alternate kinds of thinking, and political implications. These basic issues are examined against the background of Giroux's and Paul's definitions and criteria for critical thinking within a context of constructivism versus developmental and reductionist learning theories.

It seemed reasonable to me that, to get a good answer to questions about young children's ability to think critically, I needed to consult the ones who know best, the real experts - the children. During these conversations, several themes emerged. All the students were very clear about the rewards of good thinking in school -- that is, they got tangible rewards such as candy, treats or "dollars" toward Fun Friday for getting the answer right. Forgetting was a kind of "not thinking" that would land them in deep trouble. All were very much inclined to look at thinking in terms of behaviors. On the other hand, there was a definite sense that there were different kinds of thinking, that thinking could be, and often was, fun, and there was some sense of the intrinsic rewards of good thinking. Bad thinking was equated with bad behavior and the wages of this sin were many and explicit. Critical thinking, in the forms of problem solving, decision making and metacognition was highly visible.

Whether critical thinking in young children is considered from the perspective of the reasoned and rational Paul or the passionate and political Giroux, it is clear that these young children, with only six years of lived experience, most of it outside of an organized institution, have done a lot of very good critical thinking, and have developed many of the attributes of higher order thinking associated with critical thinking. Characteristics of critical thinking as denoted by both Paul and Giroux such as making decisions based on reasoned judgment, drawing independent inferences, making predictions based on evidence, finding logical cause and effect, being able to view situations from another person's perspective, finding logical strategies to solve problems, solving problems creatively, and perseverance in the face of uncertainty, are found throughout the transcripts of the children's conversations with me.

What these children are not able to do is express these skills clearly and precisely in a manner that satisfies Piaget's ideas of formal reasoning or the reductionist detailed lists. To find such skills as developing strategies for problem-solving and decision-making, for example, the researcher must listen carefully, accept the examples given by the child, and analyze them from the point of view of the child. What may seem to the reductionist theorist as unsupported and undetailed conclusions, and to the developmentalist an inability to focus on concrete facts, are, when perceived from a constructivist and critical thinking perspective, critical and creative thinking at its best. There are many examples of this in the analysis of the transcripts that follow.

Nor do the children feel politically empowered to think either independently or critically. Not only is their thinking devalued and commodified by the teachers and other adults, it is manipulated and shaped by the thinking of the teacher who empowers only herself, and rewards and punishes on the basis of how closely the thinking of her students is allied with her own.

It is in these two very important areas that school, which says that it is helping children in precisely those areas, fails them most miserably. These children's thinking in school tends to be about guessing what answer the teacher is looking for, and behaving in such a way so as not to lose dollars for Fun Friday.

And yet, in spite of school, their higher order thinking abilities are evident to the researcher who looks for them and they are engaging in some forms of metacognition. They have formulated some rather sophisticated theories about what thinking is and how it occurs and what kinds of thinking they use.

It is rather obvious that some of the children's ideas about their thinking comes from adult influence. Most of them mention concentrating as one kind of thinking, the kind that they do in school. And they discuss thinking in terms of grades and behaviors expected of them by the teacher or another adult such as repetition and practice. Their feelings of lack of control, of thinking as something that just happens almost spontaneously, whether by divine intervention or by magic, also show adult manipulation and control.

Perhaps it is because of such adult constraints that when talking about their thinking in school, the children tended to give short answers and they were concerned with saying the "right" thing, or would say "I don't know." When talking about their thinking outside of school, on the other hand, they gave example after example of their thinking strategies and theories and talked freely about how they felt about their thinking. This phenomenon was most evident after I transcribed the conversations and looked at the pages. There were places where there were just a series of one word, or very short sentences in response to a question, and other places where paragraphs were up to a half page long. When I compared the two, I found that invariably the longer responses had to do with thinking outside of school, and the shorter ones were about thinking inside the school.

The following excerpts from the transcripts illustrate in the children's own words both critical thinking elements and theories about their thinking.

Children's Definitions of Thinking

Part of the definition of critical thinking has to do with being able to analyze the kinds of thinking that have been done and evaluating whether or not the thinking is adequate for the purpose. It presupposes a more general theory of what thinking is. In defining thinking, not only did the children link it with ideas and imagination, but they also realized some relationship to the physical brain itself, that somehow the former requires the latter.

In defining thinking, D., a six-year-old boy explained, "*I think it's people thinking about stuff they wanna happen and what they think happened.*" T., a six-year-old girl, defined it as "*Using your brain,*" and "*listening.*" Another girl, A., said that for her thinking was different from imagining. She explained, "*Thinking is...can be ideas and imagining is only seeing things without needing your eyes.*"

When asked about what happens in his head when he's thinking, S. replied, "*Well, when I'm thinking my brain starts helping me, like...you know, with words.*"

Other children simply attributed the how of thinking to the realm of mystery or religion, clearly an adult influenced opinion. It seemed that for them, both the physical and metaphysical aspects of thinking were outside their realm of control and understanding. Said B.,

Um... well, yeah, you have to think a lot, and you have to have a good brain.

Me: You do? Tell me about your brain. What do you think is going on in that brain?

Well, I know it's just sitting in my head.

Me: It just sits there? What does it do when you're thinking?

I don't know...it's just tricky.

Me: Yeah, it is kind of tricky.

It's magic, to make you think.

Later in the interview, when discussing remembering, she explained the mystery through religion.

Me: What does your brain do to make you remember?

Well, it writes it up and puts it in my brain and then thinks it and I hear it.

Me: Oh. Are you thinking in words, then? Do you remember it in words that you hear?

Well, my brain doesn't really do that. God, He really does it. He makes my brain think it and I say it out.

Another child explained it this way:

Me: Are you thinking?

Yes.

Me: Tell me about that kind of thinking. Where do you think?

Your brain.

Me: What is your brain doing while you're doing that?

You try to do it, what you can do.

Me: How do you think it does that?

Jesus just made us that way.

Later in the interview, in linking the brain with thought, he explained again:

Your brain is mostly it, or like Jesus is helping you, Jesus helps you in your heart, like if you have the month is November, but it wasn't on the board, then Jesus would help you.

For him, it seemed that whatever he did not understand could be explained by invoking the religious idea that Jesus/God acts in mysterious ways to help, and that his (the child's) understanding was immaterial to the process.

A third group of children looked on the physical process of thinking as a rather mechanical one, with many inventive theories about how this is accomplished. Some theories seemed to be influenced by having had some previous knowledge of what the brain looks like, such as this child who said he knew that the brain was "humpy." Metaphors used by these children were associated with mechanical ideas, such as the movements of a machine. Asked what his brain was doing when he was thinking, N. said,

Squishing up and down. When it does that, when it goes up and down it means you're thinking. When it goes side to side it means you're not thinking.

53

Me: Okay. That's interesting. Have you ever seen a brain?

Um huh. It moves around a lot...has a lot of humps.

Me: What do you think those humps are for?

So it can move and won't be so tight all the time.

Me: What happens if your brain is tight?

You'll die.

Me: Can you make your brain squish up and down, or does it just do it?

It does it when you want to think. Like when you have a little hump and it squishes up and down where the humps are. But before you think.

Me: Can you make it do this, or does it do this by itself?

Just by itself.

In another mechanist metaphor, S. compared his brain to spinning wheels and elastic bands. As in the metaphor of the squishing humps, different movements connoted different thoughts, ways of thinking, or reversals. S. also complained about his problems when things got to going too fast and he was stretched out.

It's like a wheel, a spinning wheel or something like that.

Me: Um huh...how does that work?

It spins around, I think.

Me: Can you feel it happening?

No.

He recalled several experiences when he clearly felt out of control, and his brain was giving him problems with thinking. He relates:

...my brain was spinning real fast and I couldn't think that fast, so I did it slowly and I got it.

Me: So are you saying that when you are thinking too fast you have to make yourself slow down and that helps you concentrate maybe?

Yeah, like when I'm building a sand castle and I go real fast, and then my head just starts going real fast, and when I write my hand goes real fast, and um...when my hand goes real fast I can't write, I just go scribble-scrabble and I have to get it off with the eraser.

Me: So when you're going too fast, and your brain is going too fast, you have to make yourself slow down?

Right.

He elaborated further on his feelings of a lack of control over this process:

Hum...well...well...it ...um...does it. It just does something else. I try to get it done before it does something else.

Me: Okay. So what you're telling me is that if you stick with what your supposed to get done you get it done, but if your brain wants to do something else it's kinda hard to get it done?

Yeah, but, um...what I'm trying to say is when it's trying to do something else the other way, I do something else that away. It's like stretching something, like a rubber band, and I write so fast before it gets over there that I'm finished before it gets over there.

Me: Yeah. Do you do that very often? When you are working on your math over here and you need your brain over here to help you, and it wants to be over there, what it is that it wants to do over there?

It wants to um...it wants to make you do something else and then come back over. See my brain just stretched me one time, and, um...it went thataway and um, see, um, I had to go to one of my friends and make my head go smack just like that!

Me: Had to get your head back together, huh?

Yeah! (laughs)

Me: Is that what teachers mean when they tell you to get your act together?

(laughs) Yeah.

Me: Sometime your brain is just scattered out everywhere?

Yeah.

Again along the line of the mechanical metaphor, one of the girls speculated on how her brain works when she gets an idea, which for her is thinking. She says:

It works around and then, poof...makes an idea! And then it puts it into my imagination. Then I close my eyes for some reason, and then I see what I'm thinking.

Good and Bad Thinking

Included in the children's definitions of thinking are their ideas about good and bad thinking. It is here that the signs of teacher/adult manipulation and control are clearest. All ten children are very sure that the result of good thinking, at least in school, is getting the right answer. T. said, in response to a question about her writing thinking: "*By looking on the board and writing them right, and doing all of it correct.*" Her thinking, she says, is what makes it correct. S. says, "*When I'm doing a worksheet and it's really hard and I think of the answer and I think it's really right then I think I'm doing some really good thinking.*" T. explains further that "*...you gotta think real hard so you can get a good grade...we have this math to take home and you have to do it all right.*"

It is interesting to note that when I asked each of the students about their best thinking they talked about answering questions and being good. T. said that her best thoughts were when she was "*...listening and answering questions in math.*" D. said that his best thought today was "*Thinking about not being bad and don't listen to someone who doesn't have any dollars that's trying to get you in trouble.*" S. said his best thinking was "*Thinking on papers. I like to work.*"

Even when their best thinking occurs outside of school, it often is in response to questions. For example, S. said

My best thinking is, like, when my Dad asks me a question and he really wants me to answer it, then I do my best thinking.

Me: Wonder why that is?

Because my Dad, because he's my father and I like him.

Evidence of devaluing the thinking of the children and the commodification of their thinking in order to control it is found in the following discussions about how the children knew when they've done some good thinking. All ten defined it in terms of behavior and rewards. Said one

Thinking about what if I do it right or what if I get it wrong or how the teacher might grade them. If I might get a sad face or a check. Or an X or something like that.

Me: So are you telling me that the marks the teacher makes on your paper tell you whether or not you're thinking?

And whether sometimes I'm...um...just talking and not getting my work done...or something like that.

Me: Are you telling me that when you're not doing your work you're not thinking?

Yep.

Later in the interview, she explained further that, for her, good thinking

...means you're not talking, that you're being nice to other people, you're being good at school, you're getting all the dollars, you're earning for Friday all the time and you're being at the front of the line and you get to write down the numbers of the people who got a dollar and you...and you...and sometimes people will be good or something like that, you get to have P.E. by yourself with the P.E. teacher.

One of the boys explained that he knew he was doing good thinking when he was "...*getting a dollar and getting something from the teacher.*"

Another boy explained it this way:

Uh...well...see, you gotta do races and um...i did it, and we got the super class award.

Me: So are you saying that thinking in school is doing what people tell you to do?

Um...yeah, because, see, if you don't do what the teachers ask you to do you don't get nothing, see, sometimes we get a treat.

Clearly these children did not feel empowered to respond to the kinds of thinking and figuring out that they were able to do outside of school. For them, good thinking had few aspects of critical thinking in that it was defined and driven by adult manipulation. For them, good thinking was teacher-pleasing behavior directed toward compliance, conformity, and lack of challenge to received assumptions and the institution of school.

Motivation to be good thinkers (good in the eyes of the controlling adult) was extrinsic and at times arbitrary. There was a real reluctance to take any risks because the consequences of independent thinking, equated in their minds with bad thinking, were very real. S.N., for example, felt that thinking on his own was bad and he could remember only bad results when he tried that. He said:

Well, when I do stuff on my own I get in deep trouble. When I go outside without no shoes and sox on I get a chill, and one time when I had the glue, I...um...and after that...when I couldn't go outside and had to stay in bed...

Me: Okay. Which makes you happier, to do thinking on your own or to do something somebody tells you.

Do something somebody else tells you.

Me: Why is that?

Cause if you don't do something, its not right and you have to get a whipping with a belt...

Me: Do you like thinking?

Yes.

Me: Do you do much of it?

No.

Yet, there persists some idea that they can and do think, and that this is something that they want to do. D. put it this way:

Well I know I like thinking...I don't like to not think because when I not think I forget about what I was going to think about..."

As aware as the students were about what the significant adults in their lives called good thinking and the rewards thereof, they were even more aware of the consequences of bad thinking. S. and D. equated bad thinking with not being able to remember something, or "acting stupid."

T. was very clear about what would happen to a child who was not a good thinker. She said

Well, um...sometimes when you don't get all your work done you get a fake dollar tooken away and when you end up with zero you can't have Fun Friday and you can't get candy for doing your homework cause you wasn't being a smart thinker...so you gotta think well or they'll take some of your blood and you gotta think well so you can concentrate, and if you don't concentrate you gotta go get a shot in your finger again, then your finger will be infected. So sometimes your teacher will send a note saying whether you're being good or not being good, and if you're doing it every day the teacher will get real angry and she'll send you out in the hallway and she'll say I'm going to send a note home about your hyper thing and I'm going to talk to you about some things, and usually Ms. S. or Mrs. B. will go out in the hall with you and talk to you about some of the stories you been telling your parents and things like that and you have to get a phone call or something like that and you'll be expended

from your classes but not your school...I don't get to watch TV or read a
book or anything. All I have to do is sit there, and I be frowning...

On the other hand, in describing an incident that took place outside of the classroom, A. considered the consequences of bad thinking, rather than being punitive and imposed upon her by someone else, as a good strategy gone awry. She put it this way:

...it's a little embarrassing for me...but there's this boy in our class who
likes to run around and chase us girls and we thought we could chase
him away. So one day so we tried, and so we started out the plan, and so
he didn't do what he usually does, so we lost him! And now he is allowed
to do what he likes to do to us!

This dichotomy between in-school and out-of-school thinking continues throughout the transcripts. In-school thinking tends to be ventriloquistic, that is an echo of the teacher's thinking or the teacher's idea of what good thinking is, and is expressed in behavioral terms. Outside the classroom, however, thinking is done on the child's terms although it is not considered real thinking.

Thinking as a Political Act

Because of the lack of empowerment for critical thinking in the school situation and the manipulation of their thinking by the adults in their lives through rewards and punishments, the only area of their thinking that seemed to belong to the children was the decision whether or not to share with anyone their innermost thoughts. Two of the children expressed some reluctance about having others know about their thinking, and a third said that others could know about his thinking only if they knew what he was like. N. explained:

Me: Okay. um...do you have a lot of friends that are good thinkers?

Yep.

Me: How can you tell when they're thinking?

Cause they tell me when they want to have time out so they can think about whether they want to do this or not.

Me: Well, if I saw you sitting in a chair like you're sitting right now, could I tell if you were thinking or not?

Um... nope, not unless I tell the person looking at me what I'm like.

The other two were much more emphatic about the idea of letting someone in on their private thoughts. B. said:

Like going over to Seth's and riding his bike...and he doesn't let me. But Seth, he's selfish. He doesn't let me play with his trucks.

Me: Why doesn't he let you play with his trucks?

Cause he thinks I'm gonna take them home.

Me: How do you know what he's thinking?

Cause, um, cause he's being rude to me.

Me: Can you always tell what people are thinking by the way they act?

Yeah.

Me: Do you always say exactly what you're thinking?

Um...just this only time.

Me: You usually don't tell people what you're thinking?

No.

Me: Wonder why that is?

Well, cause no one ever asks me.

Me: Would you like for people to ask you about your thinking more often?

No.

Me: Why?

Cause I just don't like it when people know stuff about me...only my friend.

Me: I see. So you feel like your thinking is private.

Yeah, but I just don't want people to know what I'm thinking.

A. extends this idea of privacy to what she has experienced about others' thinking.
Lying as a political act to ensure privacy is not unknown to her. She said:

Me: Can you tell what other people are thinking?

No.

Me: If you talk to them a while can you tell?

*If I asked them what they are thinking they will give me a nice little
answer and then I will know.*

Me: Um huh., And do you think they will always tell you really what
they are thinking?

Sometimes they will lie.

Me: Why do you think that will happen.

Cause they are thinking something they don't want me to know.

Strategies to Help Them Think

Much of the evidence that reveals the presence of critical thinking for the
researcher is the development of strategies to do it, and conversely the lack of
strategies implies the lack of critical thinking. While the reductionist tends to
concentrate on teaching a prescribed list of strategies, often in isolation, as a
method of building toward an ability to think critically, the developmentalist waits
for the emergence of some elementary strategies in response to a prescribed task
before intervening with teaching prescribed strategies. The constructivist,
however, uses modeling and dialogue to encourage child-developed strategies that
require critical thinking on the part of the child to develop. A method akin to an
entertwined series of feedback loops encourages the emergence of child-centered

critical thinking skills, including metacognition, in a content-centered, interdisciplinary situation.

All the children have strategies to help them think. Some of these are clearly teacher-directed or adult influenced. Using their brain as a method of thinking is an example of following an adult's direction. For example, S. said, "*I use my brain...get real quiet and think.*" Later, he said

I start not talking or anything, I don't watch TV, I don't do any thing, just think what it could be.

Me: If you don't have to think hard, you can have the TV going?

Yeah. I can do it at the same time.

Other children also mention needing quiet when trying to concentrate and think. N. said:

Well, when I go to my next door neighbor where it's real quiet and tell what I want to think, and they hear it then they know what I thought right after I say it. I get a lot of peace over there, a lot of quiet.

Me: Do you need peace and quiet to think?

Uh...sometimes like when you're doing take aways, like 15 take away 20..like take away 0..I didn't know that until I got to be five...it's 15.

Me: What kind of thinking do you do when it's noisy?

I can't think at all.

On the other hand, some strategies seem to have been developed by some children in response to the experience of having to think them up, exactly the method employed in the classroom by the constructivist teacher. Notably, these strategies were developed outside the classroom, whereas the need for peace and quiet in order to concentrate came directly from the classroom. One of the girls said that when she was having trouble thinking, she used playing on her home computer to get her brain started. She also described looking for strategies to help her think, mentioning them in terms of games and problem-solving. She said:

I've got to think of what kind of strategy I should have and all that.

Me: Well, tell me about strategies? What are they?

Well, a strategy is if you're doing something you should think of what...how you should do it. A strategy would be a plan. A plan of how you are going to get something...or a few points in a game.

Me: Okay, so do you always use strategies when you think?

No.

Me: When do you not use strategies?

When I don't need to. Like if I'm reading a book, there's nothing to worry about...I just read the book. And then if I'm talking, I don't need a strategy to talk. And then when I'm thinking of food, I don't need a strategy.

Me: So, but you use strategies when you have a problem...

Yes, when I need to.

When I asked D. what he did in order to think hard, he demonstrated by rolling up his eyes and wrinkling up his forehead. But he also said

...every day I think, and at night time I write about what I was thinking about on paper, and I write down when I ended, so the next day I can look at it and start thinking again....Every time when I know I'm thinking, I just write Think, and then I write like, uh, that I ended at what I like to play and what I like to play with, that is like radios and stuff."

Student-directed thinking in the classroom took the form of reading writing. Although the thinking is somewhat on their own, the activity is teacher initiated and teacher controlled. S. says

Well, we do our journals in the morning, and we tell what is the weather. And, we, like, think what are the words that are hard to remember, like we have to remember what it was like at the bus stop or something and then we figure what the weather could be.

Kinds of Thinking

Part of critical thinking literature mentions variations in the kind of critical thinking appropriate to the content. For example, Paul (1990) discusses mathematical thinking as distinct from historical thinking. He explains this difference as one of reasoning within the logic of a discipline. Gardner (1983) discusses variations of thinking in terms of the kind of intelligence that is being brought to bear on a certain discipline, for example, kinesthetic thinking, or analytic thinking.

Overall, the students seem to be aware of at least three different kinds of thinking. The first, concentration, seems to be adult influenced and directed. The other two, dreaming, and talking, seems to be generated by the children themselves. While philosophers such as Plato and Socrates, among many, also mention dreaming and talking as effective methods of thinking, it is interesting to note that, of the three, only concentration, a teacher-directed form, is condoned within a typical reductionist classroom setting. D. mentions them most specifically:

I have to concentrate.

Me: Are thinking and concentrating kind of the same thing?

Yep.

Me: Tell me another thing thinking is just like.

Like sleeping. Cause sleeping is the same thing as dreaming. When you're dreaming you're thinking. It's in your mind and when you're thinking it's in your mind. Thinking has a picture and dreaming has a picture.

Me: That's kinda neat to think about that, isn't it! So thinking is like concentrating...

And also like listening is thinking like I'm talking right now.

Me: So you're thinking right now while we're talking?

Yep.

Later on in the interview, D. equates thinking hard with concentrating, as do the other children. T. says, "*...when I'm not thinking, I'm not concentrating.*" D. says also that even though the kind of thinking that helps him learn most is "*the talking thinking,*" the kind of thinking he does in school is "*the concentration kind...and listening to the teacher.*" He goes on to explain, "*Everybody has to be quiet to think hard in my class...So you can concentrate.*" T. talks about "*writing thinking, and reading and listening thinking.*"

A. mentions the dreaming kind of thinking when she says, "*Well, sometimes when I'm asleep I dream about what I was thinking.*" When B. was asked when she did the most thinking, she said it was while she was sleeping, and that dreams are what make her think while she is asleep.

These theories about thinking while dreaming bear epistemological links to learning theories that speak of reflection as a necessary component of both critical thinking and understanding. Dewey (1910) explains that "We reflect in order that we may get hold of the full and adequate significance of what happens." (p. 119) The kinship with visualization is also apparent. John-Steiner (1985) relates the story of Einstein who visualized himself as a beam of light streaking through the cosmos, a dream that eventually became his theory of relativity. She quotes mathematician Morris Kline, "When one is mentally relaxed, ideas seem to come more freely as one works. In this state many possible approaches or at least ideas that should be looked into because they may bear fruit occur." (p. 182) Talking as a method of thinking critically about an issue is perhaps best understood as Socratic dialogue. That it is still valued is illustrated in a discussion cited by John-Steiner in which psychologist Irwin Maltzman describes how he generates some of his ideas:

Most of the things that I think of that are any good happen when I talk. For instance, when I give a graduate seminar and I pretty well know what I am going to talk about, I may get a new idea while I am lecturing. It might be triggered off by the overall topic or task which produces within me a wealth of associations. (John-Steiner, p. 190)

Thinking in Content Areas

Thinking within the logic of a discipline not only differentiates the discipline and allows understanding of it as a discrete body, but it also defines the process that leads to this understanding. Thus, there is a symbiotic relationship between discovering the logic and understanding the discipline that is best processed through the medium of critical thinking. That is, discovering the strategies that will lead to an understanding of the logic of a discipline will at the same time uncover the process whereby the logic can be understood. For example, using the strategy of looking for patterns in mathematics not only uncovers the patterns that are there but also leads to an understanding of the way that patterns function in providing a mathematical solution to mathematical problems.

In asking about the kinds of thinking they did in school as far as content is concerned, S. differentiated between mathematical thinking and thinking in words. He said,

Well, thinking in math is, that, you know what the math problem is and you're not thinking what the sound of a letter is. You're thinking of...well, sometimes a person might be putting a number in your head and counting up.

Me: Okay. What kind of thinking do you do when you're reading?

You think of what the sounds are, then you put them together and find out what the word is. And you start reading.

D. explains it this way:

If I need to get some number thinking done, like is it twenty or thirty, or forty, and when I look at either one or two or how much I need, or how much letters it has in it, and how much, that means how much unifix cubes I need, and when I look at the unifix cubes it helps me think better...I can draw numbers with my finger, and look at it and say, "Now I got it!"

Me: Tell me what you do when you see a group of letters and you've never seen that word before.

I think, and then I ask mom, and if she doesn't know it, then I think some more. And if I got it then I write it on my paper if I have to and if I don't ...um...

Me: What are some of the things you think about in order to get it?

Like, stuff like if it has a T, or D, or R in it then I think that if it has something in it like that then what rhymes with that word, then I think of that and I say to my mom that I have it.

Many of the students mentioned the value of practice and repetition in helping them think and remember in school, both in reading and math. N. puts it this way:

Me: When you're doing your math like your numbers and everything and you have to add some numbers together, do you have to think to do that?

No, I just know it right away.

Me: Oh. How do you know something?

Cause I've been practicing.

Me: So before you practiced you didn't know it?

Um huh.

Me: And after you practiced you did know it?

Yeah.

Me: How do you know the difference when you don't know it and when you do?

Cause, um...you know I was practicing I was using my fingers.

Me: And what happened then?

Then I found out.

Me: So what did you do with your fingers after you found out.

I didn't use my fingers no more.

Me: And that's how you knew that you knew?

Yeah.

S. describes an incident that occurred when he was an infant in which repetition helped him learn something. He relates:

Like a long long time ago when I was a baby, I fell out of my baby crib! (laughs) into the basket head first. My mom had to put me back in the crib and I did it again, and again, so she put me in my baby bed and I couldn't get out!

Me: So, are you saying that if something bad happens over and over again, that makes you remember?

Yes.

Me: So you had to think to remember not to fall out of your baby bed?

Yes.

Me: What if something good happens to you over and over again? would that help you remember?

Yes. when I was swimming I tried and.. and when you try you get better and better, so I tried, and when I did all I could, I started to swim, so I could, there was a jumping board, and I jumped off the jumping board.

He also said that repetition helps him study, for example in spelling.

Well, in spelling we got this paper, this spelling word paper, my mom has to write them down, I have to write them down, and uh...and my mom has to write them down, so when I go to school the next day, I got a 100 on my paper.

And N. also relies on the same strategy for learning to read. He says, "*I'd keep on doing it over and over until I get it right.*"

I also asked about scientific thinking: Were they doing any of that?

D. said, "*What's science?*" I said "You know, like learning about rocks or animals..." He replied, "*We don't study anything like that.*" S. was similarly emphatic. "*I don't study science. What is science?*"

Of the ten students interviewed, only one mentioned thinking in science, and that was in connection with a rock collection that he had at home.

Uh...my science thinking? We only do math. And reading.

Me: You don't study rocks or animals and things?

I study rocks at home.

Me: Tell me about your thinking when you're studying rocks.

I think about if there's any dirt that needs to be cleaned, or if it's stepped on and chipped off or broken, if I can glue it, and I say "I take this back and find another one just like it."

Me: Can you find another one?

Yep. I take it back and get another one. I have my very first rock.

Me: What kind is that?

It's black with gray dots.

It is noteworthy that this one mention of scientific thinking incorporates the critical thinking skills of compare and contrast (noting details so as to find another rock like the one he has), problem-solving (what to do about the broken or dirty rock), and the complementary attitudes of intellectual curiosity and caring enough about something to take the time to investigate. It is also worth noticing that many constructivist teachers, Eleanor Duckworth as a foremost example, use the world around the child to teach all the skills necessary for learning and understanding.

A constructivist teacher would use the curiosity of the child about animals, plants, rocks and stars to stimulate an interest in reading and math. Teaching those skills which often become drudgery otherwise within the framework of science gives a child-directed reason for learning them. Only in a reductionist classroom would a teacher require mastery of all the individual skills of reading and math before allowing any branching out into the wonderful world outside. Unfortunately, the reductionist method of teaching is dominant, not only because of the dominant interest in maintaining the status quo, but also because it is easily tested, graded and requires little skill or thinking on the part of poorly trained (and poorly compensated) teachers.

Thinking Outside of School

It is interesting to note that important critical thinking skills such as making predictions, problem solving, using their background knowledge to clarify and ascertain the reliability of information, discovering logical cause and effect, and using critical thinking to modify behavior take place outside of the school setting. However, these skills are not considered by the children as "really thinking." They realize that they are doing some thinking, but because it is seen as necessary as in the instance of thinking to learn to ride a bicycle, or fun as in playing games, it isn't important enough to be included in the "really thinking" category. For example:

Me: I'm interested in what you said about thinking when you're working and thinking when you're playing. You said you liked thinking when you're working. Tell me about the difference in those kinds of thinking.

Because I like to learn, you know, so I like to do lots of work so I'll learn.

Me: So when you're playing, you're not learning?

No, I'm learning what to build, like Legos, you know.

Me: What about when you're learning to ride a bicycle. Is that thinking and learning?

I know when I learned to ride a bicycle what I was thinking about. Trying to think about keeping my balance so I won't tip over and about not going over a lot when I'm turning...See, mom was helping me and when I would start to tip over, my mom would come over and help me. One time I went around for a long time before I started to tip over...

Me: Did you have to think real hard to learn to ride a bicycle?

Yes, sort of.

Me: Is that a harder kind of thinking than doing a worksheet where you already know the answers?

No...Yeah...Sort of...

Me: Well, suppose you were learning to ride a bicycle and you were doing some really good thinking, could you use that same kind of good thinking in the classroom to do a worksheet?

No.

Me: Why not?

Because they're different. Like learning to ride a bicycle you have to think how to keep your balance and stuff. When you're doing a worksheet, you're thinking of...like four plus four and stuff...

T. talks about thinking that helps her learn to ride her bicycle:

...sometimes I have to get my wheels tooken off so I can learn how to ride without training wheels and sometimes I'll fall and I have to ..have to start over and I start thinking.

D. also talks about thinking and doing something, in his case, ice skating.

...At the skating rink if you think about it and you skate at the same time then its easy, but if you don't think about it at the skating rink and you skate then you'll always fall.

Problem Solving

Not only is problem-solving a critical thinking skill itself, but it is also a way of developing critical thinking skills. It includes identifying the problem, recognizing the information given that is necessary to finding a solution, being able to find information that is missing or to state that the problem is not solvable in its present form, developing strategies and evaluating those strategies as to their relative value in solving the problem, making predictions based on alternate strategies that might be used, and recognizing implications resulting from the implementation of strategies.

Although problem-solving was not cited by the children as a way of thinking in the classroom, it was frequently mentioned outside the school as necessary to their lived experiences. I asked S., "How do you go about solving problems?" He first had to think up a problem, and when he did it had to do with a problem outside of school. He described helping his friends learn to stop fighting and play with each other, but when asked if that was when he did his best thinking, he said that happened when he was doing a worksheet. D. described the following problem solving episode:

> We've got these little firecracker things, and I have to think where I can drop them, because we have this carpet, and Mom said that if we threw them in the house we'd start a fire in there on the carpet so I have to think where I can throw them even in the bathroom, so I have to go outdoors and throw them in the road. Or I can throw them on the steps or in front of the fireplace where the wood is hard.

N. described using his best thinking to figure out how to keep from getting hurt when he was doing his chores. He said:

Me: When do you do the most thinking?

Uh...when I'm doing my work...actually my chores.

Me: Tell me about your chores.

I gotta pick up trash in the back yard.

Me: Okay. What kind of thinking do you have to do to get that done?

Uh...some fast thinking.

Me: Like about what?

Uh...picking...like when I was a kid I skinned myself on a glass bottle and you could see my bones inside my hand.

Me: So, are you telling me then that when you pick up trash you have to think about what you're picking up?

Yeah.

Me: So you don't hurt yourself?

Yeah, like I did when I was a little baby.

T.'s descriptions of her thinking at home included stories about coming up with strategies to deal with looking after her sister and brother while her mother was gone, as well as ways to clean the house, fix food for herself and her siblings, and how to get someone else to take over the babysitting when it got to be too much for her. Using thinking to modify her own behavior was a part of this. She said, "*Well...sometimes I'm thinking we better not do that because we'll get in trouble...*" And later, she said, "*I was like, whoops, I'm gonna quit this stuff, and I did.*"

When S. described a game of hide-and-seek with friends he talked about thinking about the rules of the game, about what role each would play and about strategies he had for not getting caught. He said, "*Sometimes, I'm thinking, like, I can't get too close because he might find me. And then I think of a place.*" Asked when he had the most fun thinking, he said, "*When we're playing a game and I'm thinking really hard where I can hide.*"

Using their skills of making predictions based on evidence and logical cause and effect seemed to be an everyday occurrence outside of school. T. talks about having to think ahead about what her younger siblings might want to do in order to be able to circumvent any possible accidents, and all of them discuss these strategies being used in games with other children.

Evaluating Reliable Sources

The critical thinking skill of using background information to assess the validity of information or truth claims is one that reductionists say cannot be used by young children because they do not recognize the validity of the lived experiences of the children. This is a political attitude that recognizes only the approved experiences, that is, the experiences of the dominant power. Not only does this say that dominant experiences are valid, but also that the lived experiences of the children, unless they occurred in school under the supervision of the teacher, cannot be used to assess the reliability of the source of information. However, most of the children had discovered the strategy of using past experiences and background knowledge to evaluate the reliability of sources of information. And they used this skill both in school and out of school. For example, B. talks about a classmate who tries to get her to believe what she is telling her. She said:

> Um...this girl, her name is --- and she lies to me and I know she is lying
> because she doesn't have that much money. And sisters...she says she had
> 83 sisters.

Me: What kind of thinking do you have to do to know she is lying?

Well, cause no one in the world can't have 80 sisters!

And later, she uses the same strategy of calling on previous knowledge to help her with her reading.

Me: Have you ever read something in a book that sounded a   little strange, and you think maybe its not true?

Yeah. I think "photo" is "poto" because it starts with a 'p' and that's weird.

Me: Yeah.

And strange!

Me: So are you comparing what you know about the letter 'p' with the word you see?

Yeah, but 'photo' really starts with a 'f'...

Yellow it sounds like a 'e' but they really made it a 'y' and they made it like it sounds like it starts with a 'a' but it doesn't, it starts with a 'e'.

Me: So when things get confusing you go back to what you know already?

Yeah.

A. describes this incident in which she used the same strategy to discern the truth.

Me: Let me ask you about this. When someone says something to you and you're trying to decide if its true or not, what do you think about to let yourself know whether or not its true?

Well, first I've got to think if anyone has had that happen, like if that happened to me once. So if someone said to me I've got a pet unicorn I wouldn't believe them because no one's had a pet unicorn. And then if someone said I've got $30 or $20 and I can spend a few dollars, I'd say that's true.

Me: So what you're saying is when somebody says something or you hear something or read it in a book you compare it with what you already know to decide if its true?

Yes.

N. also was able to recall a time when he used this strategy to help him solve a problem.

Me: Suppose you got a really really hard problem that was taking you a long time to figure out, what kind of thinking would you have to do in math?

Um...number thinking, just like one, two, three, four, five, six, seven...10 plus 10 is twenty and that...

Me: But suppose you had to figure out something like...suppose you had ten cows and then you got five more cows...

that would be fifteen.

Me: ... but then somebody bought six of your cows...how many would you have left?

bought six of 'em? I'd have nine.

Me: How did you figure that out?

I just thought real fast.

Me: But what did you think?

Uh..like when I was a little kid and my next door neighbor had nine cats and now he has two, and three dogs and one of them died.

Me: So it helps you if you remember something from before?

Um huh.

Suspension of Logic for Television Watching

Discovering logical cause and effect is a necessary component for many kinds of critical thinking. In analyzing decision-making situations, in recognizing implications of implementing certain strategies, in seeing what necessarily does or does not follow a statement, the skill of logical cause and effect is indispensable. And, by implication, recognizing logical cause and effect is also needed in order to recognize its opposite, illogical cause and effect. Nowhere is this more clearly called for than in the world of television. Not only in advertising is it needed, but also within the programs themselves.

For the children, television presents a special problem. Most all of them said that watching television did not require thinking but instead called for a suspension of logic, which conversely implies that all of them had some clear understanding of the logic of cause and effect. D. and I had this conversation:

Me: Do you ever do any thinking while you're watching TV?

Um..like thinking how the cartoon should be. Like Darkwing Duck, it should be, ...like refrigerators killing you.

Me: Are refrigerators killing you?

Yeah, like to see the shocking man that can start a frigerator. Well, um, if refrigerators are going to be killing him, it should be when Darkwing turns around, not when he goes Whoooo, Whooo, and then it can jump up the wall. Because when Darkwing turns around, the refrigerator jumps up and stays up in the air, and when Darkwing turns around, he says "I swore I saw a refrigerator there," and then when he turns again, it falls on his head.

Me: Um hum. And you think that's not the way it ought to be?

No.

Me: Are you saying that you're doing better thinking than the people who wrote the...

Yeah, because it's much more better, much more funnier. I bet no one laughs at that cartoon cause its not funny a bit. I don't even laugh at it cause I like my thinking.

Me: So are you saying that if you were doing the thinking behind the cartoon, you'd like for it to be a little more logical type of thinking rather than have just surprises?

Yeah.

Decision Making

Decision-making is not only a part of the problem-solving process, but it is also a critical thinking skill within itself. It involves recognizing whether or not enough information is on hand to make a decision, considering creative alternatives, and considering implications of implementing decisions. It also involves prioritizing input as to its importance to the desired outcome of the decision.

One of the most used techniques for making decisions discussed by the children was that of considering many possibilities and basing the decision on what seemed best at the time. For example, when asked about how she decided what to draw, B. explained:

Um...well...um...you think in your mind...and you just think everything in the world, like, the world, space ship, rainbow...all that stuff...or something...

Me: Okay. You're thinking all these thoughts...how do you decide which one you're going to put on paper?

Think which one is the best and which one I'm gonna do.

S. also looks at possibilities before making decisions. He says that before deciding what toys he wants to play with, he looks at all the toys he has and then decides what to play.

Another decision making skill that was apparent was that of weighing the consequences before making the decision. This was used by a number of children. A. relates:

I think about it, if it would be a good idea or a bad...if it's a bad idea then I let go of it.

Me: That's probably a good idea. What sort of things do you think about to decide if its good or bad?

Well, I've got to think of...if...I should really do it...if its a joke then...if its doing something to someone I don't think it would be a very good one...if it's a joke that I can say out, then I have to think about how to say it and how the person whose in it would feel.

Me: Okay, so you think what may happen after you do something to decide if its a good idea.

Yes.

B. describes the process she used one night when she and two little friends had to decide whether to spend the night in the backyard in a tent or come inside. She told me:

I thought that they would pick to go sleep in the tent and they didn't. I didn't either.

Me: Why didn't you all want to sleep in the tent?

There's 2 reasons. The tent was too little, but we could still fit in and I could sleep a different way. And us, there's rats in their house so they make traps.

Me: Oh. So let me make sure I understand this process. When you and N and M get together you decide what you want to do, you have a good idea and you think about the reason you should or shouldn't do that?

Yeah.

Me: And then you make a decision whether or not to do what you thought about?

Yeah. Or getting scared, really scared at night, with the tent and the rats coming. I really hate rats!

Putting Themselves in Another's Place

Reciprocity, or being able to empathetically think about what another person might be thinking is necessary in many areas of critical thinking. Not only it is used in discovering the logic of an opposing point of view, it is also necessary to an understanding of alternate solutions or perspectives on an issue. It is a prime component of historical thinking, of scientific thinking, of thinking critically about a painting, a piece of music or literature, or indeed in any situation where deeper understanding requires understanding the motives and perspective of another person.

Here again, even though this skill is recognized as prime among critical thinking skills, most of the examples cited by the children were those from outside the classroom. For example, one of T.'s most frequently used thinking skills is to be able to put herself is her sibling's place and think like they might be thinking in order to anticipate what they might do or want next, so she can be prepared to deal with the situation. In a less stressful situation, B. has found that in order to anticipate the needs of her kitten, she must also put herself in its place. And she is able to very quickly give another very good example of thinking what another person might be thinking.

Me: What kind of thinking do you do when you're working with your kitten?

Well...to look after it and not let the dogs get it and keep it inside and lift it up and help it where it wants to go.,..like it thinks her mom is up on one of the counters in the tack room, and I let her do that.

Me: Okay. So you have to kinda think what the kitten may be thinking. Is that what you're doing? You're putting yourself in the kitten's place...Do you ever do that with people?

Yeah.

Me: Tell me about that.

Um..me and my friend, we play I spy, and um, and when she says I spy something green and I say the tree, and she says no, and uh, then I say the grass, and she says yes.

A. uses the technique in reading, not necessarily in school, in order to understand more about what she is reading. She explained:

I think...um...if it's real funny I think how the person who wrote it thought. I try to think of that, and if it's real sad I think how sad that person was feeling. And then if it's happy I think of happiness and the person who is writing it...between all that. And in between I think that person is a very strange thinker.

Words Vs. Pictures

Both Gardner (1983) and John-Steiner (1985) talk about the many ways that people think. John-Steiner cites many examples, most notably that of Einstein, of visualization of concepts, and Gardner talks of spatial intelligence. Although this distinction is not addressed per se in critical thinking theory, it is important as a component of the way young children learn. To assume that, because a child is not a logical/mathematical or analytical learner, critical thinking skills cannot be used is not using thinking skills on the part of the teacher. Critical thinking skills can be used in any of the intelligence areas. They are not content specific, nor are they hierarchical. That is, critical thinking in mathematics is not more critical than critical thinking in literature or music.

Most of the children that I interviewed described thinking in pictures rather than in words. A., for example, said

Me: Are you thinking in words or pictures?

Well, it's little pictures, moving around, doing what my idea is.

And later in the interview, she said:

Me: Okay, you said that when you think, you saw little pictures in your head. Are they in color or black and white?

Color.

Me: Okay. What kind of colors do you think in?

Well, there's ...um...there's the colors that those creatures and all those things are in.

Me: What about the unicorns?

Well, then I see it in white.

Me: Oh. Are all unicorns white?

Some can be pink, black or any color.

Me: But yours are white?

I like them white.

N. also is very sure that he thinks in pictures rather than in words. He says:

Me: When you're reading are you thinking in pictures or in words?

The pictures. I just look at the pictures and then read the sentences.

Me: So the pictures kind of help you read the words?

Um huh.

Me: How would you read the words if you didn't have any pictures with them?

Uh...I'd just try the words...comparing it to writing.

Me: Okay. Do you ever have pictures in your head when you're just seeing words?

Yeah.

Me: Does that help?

Some. Yeah.

Me: Okay. When ..Do you get the pictures in your head after you've said the word?

No, Before. I just look at the word and then think what it is and then say the word.

On the other hand, in discussing how she remembers things, B. explained that:

Me: What does your brain do to make you remember?

Well, it writes it up and puts it in my brain and then thinks it and I hear it.

Thinking with the Body

Other children described ways of thinking that Howard Gardner (1983) would call kinesthetic, that is thinking in movement, and some talked about using their ears to think. A., for example, describes playing the piano as an activity that requires not only her sight, but her ears and her fingers. She says:

I've got to think of which note, which keys are which notes, and which notes should I press at which time.

Me: Um huh. So when you see the notes on paper...

Yeah, I've got to press it, I've got to press the keys with my finger, play real good and fast.

Me: Okay...when you do that, are you thinking with your eyes or your fingers or your ears?

All.

Me: Um hum. If you put cotton in your ears, could you still play the piano?

No, cause I wouldn't be able to hear if the song was right.

Me: But if you're reading the notes on the paper and you're pressing the right keys with your fingers, would that not tell you that it was right?

But it might be at the wrong...it could be at the wrong tune.

Me: Oh, at the wrong place on the piano you mean?

Yes, the wrong tune.

Me: Okay, so you need all three.

Yes.

Me: Well, do you ever use your body to think with?

Yes.

Me: When do you do that?

Sometimes I got to use my body when I'm running. Cause I can slide around outside on poles, and I got to jump and I have to..I can also...And I've got to use my body to help me practice my arms and legs and head to move.

Me: Okay. So that's the kind of thinking you're doing then...making your body move.

Yes.

Me: Is it harder making your body move or to play the piano?

I think...when I'm playing the piano.

Me: Why?

Cause I'm very new at it, and with running...my body has been in use for years.

When I asked N. if he ever thought with his body, he replied, "*My brain and my feet.*" He explained:

Me: Are you telling me you are thinking with your feet?

Like...uh..drawing pictures. you can draw on the floor if you pretend your toes are pencils.

Me: Um huh. Do you ever think dancing with your feet?

Yep. I just go tapping, tapping like that.

Me: So moving around helps you think. Is that what you're telling me?

Yep.

Me: Moving your fingers and moving your feet. Do you think better when you're moving or sitting still?

Moving.

And on another occasion, he said:

Me: Do you ever think in movements? Like if you close your eyes and think about skating, could you feel yourself skating?

Yep.

Me: Could you feel what you need to do to skate?

Uh...when I wanted to learn, I just closed my eyes, I wanted to know, to feel how it needed to be to skate, to learn how, and I just closed my eyes and I felt myself moving because I was holding myself with one hand and trying to do a trick, and I felt my feet moving.

Me: Were your feet moving?

Nope, but I felt them jiggling for real.

Because children think in these many ways that they can describe, it is necessary for critical thinking theory to address these ways in some form. Whether it is to incorporate these ways of learning into the skills such that they modify and adapt the skills to their primary mode of perception, or to simply recognize them as valid ways of learning, it is important that the teacher of young children recognize the problem and look for viable solutions. Here again, reductionist and developmental teaching methods fall short when compared with a constructivist method. Where the reductionist would insist on reducing all critical thinking to a programmatic set of skills to be mastered in a particular way by everyone regardless of way of learning, and the developmentalist would wait until mode of learning as well as development of concepts is seen through prescribed testing, the constructivist would encourage the diversity of critical thinking applications that the many ways of learning develop without waiting for them to be prescribed by the teacher or a programmatic curriculum. That the children think in those diverse ways is reason enough to encourage and facilitate their happening. For the constructivist classroom, divergent thinking, critical dialogue and creativity would be the prevalent attitude.

Summary

In this analysis of the conversations with these children, I have shown that the major elements of critical thinking are present when young children tell about their thinking. Not only can they talk about their thinking, but they demonstrate unmistakably that such thinking is being used. The criteria of both Paul and Giroux, when applied to what these children have to say about their thinking, show that they are met when analyzed from the perspective of the world of the child rather than the expectations of adults. Such skills as problem-solving, decision-making, reciprocity, developing strategies, recognizing logical cause and effect, compare and contrast, and making predictions based on evidence are present with many examples.

These skills, however, are more often used outside the classroom than within it, and seem to have developed because of the demands of their lived experiences not through the instruction of the classroom teacher. They have developed within the many diverse ways of learning and understanding that all children have, not just within the framework of the logical/mathematical intelligence.

In Chapter Five, I will develop the conclusions and the implications of this study, and lay the groundwork for further research in to critical thinking in early childhood.

CHAPTER FIVE

CONCLUSIONS

If the business of the school is to help students become competent critical thinkers, and both Paul and Giroux would agree that it is, then the earlier such thinking is begun in the schools the better are the prospects for being successful at it. Unfortunately, school seems to be the one place where critical thinking not only is not encouraged, but is often discouraged in the pursuit of trivia and facts, and under the auspices of control. John Barell addressed this when he wrote:

We, the adults, do more to stifle students' thinking than perhaps any other element I could identify. We do this by the kind of problem we do not present students to solve and by the ways in which we respond to students' answers or comments. We control by making all the decisions about what is to be learned, how, when, where, why, and what grade to put on it after it is over.

It is, therefore, necessary to emphasize from the very first day of school that this is *our classroom:* Here we work together toward common goals. Here everybody has some responsibility for his/her learning and for that of others as well. Students will not and cannot feel empowered if everything is done for and to them. If they have no opportunity to set goals, design strategies, and feel responsible for these decisions, they will

leave school with less than a feeling of confidence in their own ability to
take control of their own lives. (Barell, p. 70-71)

And if our students are to become empowered to take control of their own lives,
teachers and schools must allow them to become competent at controlling
themselves and their education. Thus the supremely political act that Giroux .
envisions has a chance to make major changes in injustice, to challenge the status
quo that so endangers the future of our students. The danger is not that our
students will not be able to get a job when they graduate. It is that they will not
be able to think, that they will not be able to change to cope with a chaotic and
changing society, that they will have no idea who or where they are.

Children Are Already Thinking Critically

Conversations such as I had with young children confirm what Barell, Paul,
Giroux, Duckworth and many others say: That young children are already
thinking critically. The problem is that they do it privately, or they do it when
they don't think adults will notice, at play for example, or when they are forced to
take on adult roles at home. They seem to have a nagging feeling that it's
something they ought not to be doing, and yet they don't seem to be able to stop.
Until, however, they come to school and the teachers train them very carefully not
to. In school, they come to devalue real thinking themselves, and take rote
memorization as their own definition of thinking. Instead of letting them ask
questions and wonder about the answers they find, instead of helping them learn,
they are taught. Taught to wait quietly, color in the lines, find the "right answer"
and not to cheat by telling anyone else what you know. And they are rewarded
with "fake dollars" for Fun Friday, dollars and fun that are as fake as the
education we are assaulting them with.

Changing the Classroom Environment

In response to what I learned from young children about their thinking, I looked at many aspects of my own early childhood classroom. I began with the physical environment, and focused on barriers to critical thinking. For example, I looked at materials for the children that would encourage experimenting and talking, as well as creative risk-taking. As I looked around the classroom, I made some major changes.

One of the first things I removed from the classroom were labels. In the block center, for example, it was recommended that I put pictures on the shelves showing which blocks belonged there. The thinking was that this would help the children begin to understand categories. What I wanted them to do, however, was understand categories by developing them on their own using categories that were meaningful to them. In the same way, I removed labels from other centers, and removed restrictions about carrying materials from center to center. Thus, when blocks were needed for cooking, or a baking sheet from the kitchen was needed for a roof, or sand and water for a cake in the kitchen, the children were free to use the materials in any way that they wished. Instead of making clean-up time harder, my instructions were for them to put them where they belonged (not in the center where I had put them, necessarily) so that they had to do a certain amount of deciding what "belonging together" meant. A criticism of this technique was that the children needed the labels, not only for categories, but also to become aware of print communication. To answer this, I made sure that print media was present in every center. There were books such as Changes, Changes in the block center, books about animals, plants and such in the science center, menus from restaurants and cookbooks in the kitchen, books about boats and sandcastles in the sand and water play area.

I also wanted to be sure that a large variety of materials were available to the children for their use every day. That necessitated putting materials within easy reach and empowering the children to get them as they needed them. It also gave them the responsibility of using only what they needed, of sharing with others, and taking care of the supplies. The critical thinking goals of planning and devising strategies were reinforced here.

To make sure that each of the centers appealed to as many of the five senses as possible, I added some things not usually found in early childhood classrooms. For example, although science centers generally have many plants in them, I wanted plants that appealed not only to sight, but also to smell, touch and taste. Mints of several varieties with fuzzy leaves, oregano, lemon basil, chives, and other herbs were perfect for this. We could compare not only the different shapes but also the variety of scents and tastes. Some leaves were shiny and smooth, others were fuzzy or soft, and hues ranged from light to dark. Simply experimenting with and getting to know the variety of tastes, sights, smells, and feels stimulated thinking and talking in the science center. I also added sound boxes to the science center made with natural materials such as rocks, seeds, sand, leaves, and twigs. An insect zoo populated with buzzing. chirping, hopping, crawling and flapping bugs caught in the vicinity of the school helped with the sounds. We also had a cockateil, a parakeet, several fish, some crabs, a couple of African frogs, some salamanders, some American chameleons, a hamster, a guinea pig and a rabbit.

In the kitchen center, we added cinnamon sticks, herbs from the science center, perfume and powder for dress-up, scented soaps for clean-up, and a radio. However, we had no pretend plastic food for the same reason we deleted the labels. A plastic hamburger is always a plastic hamburger, but a couple of blocks can be a sandwich or a cake (and you can use crayons for the candles) or whatever you choose to call it. An empty plate can have on it whatever you choose to say is on it. Imagination is part and parcel of good critical thinking, and while props can help stimulate thinking they should not take the place of it.

In the reading center, all the books had a special, three-dimensional object to go with it. Puppets, dolls dressed like the characters in the book, flannelboard cutouts to go with the story, even a special pillow to cuddle while reading were included. Many of the books also had tapes to listen to while looking and playing with the dolls and things.

My goal was to stimulate as much conversation, as much curiosity, as much inquiry as possible through the presentation of the materials and arrangement of the environment as could be done, appealing not only to the five senses but also to Gardner's (1983) seven intelligence areas.

Instructional Methods

Not only did I change the physical environment in response to the study of how and when young children think, I also changed my methods of instruction. I wanted to make sure that it was the child's interaction with the material and what each child came to understand about basic concepts because of this interaction that was the focus, not what I, as an adult, chose to have them understand about what they were experiencing. My role as a teacher also changed, from directing and teaching the child to providing experiences for the child such that basic concepts necessary for an understanding of the world could be uncovered by the child during the interaction with the materials and discussing them.

For example, to encourage children to learn to make predictions, many teachers' manuals suggest that children guess what is going to happen next in a story, or a similar activity. However, guessing is not the same as making predictions or making reasoned judgements. So instead of simply saying, "What do you think is going to happen?" I also ask for details that they have found in the text that make them think that.

In my early childhood classroom, a favorite book is Eric Carle's Do You Want To Be My Friend? On the first page is a little mouse asking, "Do you want to be my friend?" Also on the page is part of an animal. Thus, when I ask, "Who do you think he is talking to?" I follow it by another question: "What do you see in the picture that makes you think that?" On several pages, (for example on the page after the hippopotamus), there is room for real debate (as to whether the animal is a fish or a bird). I also have on hand several animal books so we can check them for details about what a fish or bird looks like. Sometimes we take a long time to talk about the possibilities, and this is important. Critical thinking -- in this case, making predictions based on details within the text --is necessarily time consuming. As John Barell (1991) has explained, there can be no shortcuts when teaching for thoughtfulness is the goal.

Using Socratic discussion as a tool for fostering critical thinking is important at any age, and even young children can participate. Talking about manners, classroom rules, or negotiating through disagreements can all be positive learning experiences that call for critical thinking on the part of the students if they are entered into with the idea of empowering students to make a difference in the way the classroom is run. For example, I learned to help students settle their own grievances through discussion rather than take it upon myself to impose a solution. Through this procedure, the student learns to look at the problem from another person's perspective, to consider alternative ways of solving the problem, to explore the consequences of possible solutions, and to evaluate those solutions that were chosen. I am also giving them the necessary authority to make these decisions and to solve these problems.

I learned to listen to what my students were saying and to try to understand the underlying understandings that they were bringing to a situation. This gave me insight into what materials and experiences I needed to set before them in order to clear up misunderstandings and confusions. For example, one of my students, Chris, complained to me one day that there were three people on the climbing cube. The cube is quite small, and there is room for only two, and we had talked about the reasons for limiting the number of people on it. However, when I looked, I saw only two students there. I almost said, "No, there are only two." I knew he could count quite well, however, so I wondered what the real question was. So, instead, I said, "Tell me what you mean." He explained, "Well, Tami and Takiyah were on the bottom, and that was two, but then Tami got on top." I waited for a minute, and then he said, "and that makes three." So, I said, "Let's go over there and talk about this a little." When we went over, I asked Tami and Takiyah to help us with a problem. We counted the girls as they were both on the bottom, one on bottom and one on top, both on top, naming and counting as we went. Finally Chris was satisfied that the number of students didn't change as the girls moved around, and I realized that I needed to provide him with more conservation activities until he really understood the concept of conservation of number. Listening to his thinking helped me realize the underlying misunderstanding and to ask the right questions to help him in his struggle to make sense of a discrepancy that he was experiencing. Had I been intent only on teaching, I would have never had any insight into his thinking, nor would I have been able to demonstrate to him that thinking through a problem is truly a worthwhile activity. Part of beginning critical thinking is finding the necessity for it, claiming it as a worthwhile endeavor, giving the time for it, and empowering the students to do it.

Paley addresses this same issue in her writing about her early childhood classroom. She says,

This is not too much time to give to words and their meaning. The children learn that figuring out what we do and say and read and play are equally important. Everything is supposed to make sense; if it doesn't, ask questions, go over it again, find out why the picture is blurred. The range of possibilities for misunderstandings is quite astonishing. And is this not a lucky circumstance? It means we ought never to run out of great curriculum materials, free for the asking. We only need to listen for our own errors and there is enough text to fill the school year. (Paley, p. 48-9)

Another part of critical thinking of major importance is taking the time to help the student understand the kind of thinking that was going on as he figured something out. Talking with the very youngest children is one way, recommended by such philosophers as Dewey (1991) and Barell (1991). For first graders and older, Vygotsky (1986) recommends writing for figuring out thinking. He explains that, "Writing...requires deliberate analytical action on the part of the child...Written language demands conscious work because its relation to inner speech is different from that of oral speech." (Vygotsky, p. 182) With young children, however, talking is a necessary beginning. Making the link between oral speech and inner speech begins the process of thinking while talking. Writing as a method of thinking through an issue will naturally follow as the child begins to write, even though the relationship with inner speech is different. Then, with writing, the relationship is, as Vygotsky implies, more consciously formed, but it serves the same function of making the thinking clearer and more focused for the writer.

One example of this can be found in a method of teaching metacognition that I use in the block center. I may begin to build a tower, deliberately putting the larger blocks on top. The children are playing alongside me, listening as I talk to myself about what I am doing. I say, "I'm building a tower. Putting these little ones here, now it's getting taller and taller, and this big one can go right here...uh, oh, it fell down. Now, I wonder why? Maybe I can make it wider at the bottom. Or I might not make it tall. I wonder what will happen if I use the big blocks first and the little ones last?" I try out all of these possibilities, not necessarily deciding which one is best, just building the towers, and talking about what I want to do, what I think might have been not a good idea that I did that keeps me from getting a tall tower, and trying out several solutions. Soon, my students are using this same technique of talking among themselves or to themselves about their thinking and about whether or not it was sound thinking.

My experience in this area is not unique. Other teachers of young children also tell about many conversations with their students during which fairly sophisticated theories about their thinking were expressed. John Barell tells about a situation in a first grade classroom when he called on the students to solve a problem and then to explain how they went about figuring out how to solve it. He relates:

One girl, Betsy, said, "I remembered what we did at home [in a similar situation]." So Betsy was using her background knowledge, and her comment convinced me that some youngsters, even first graders, could reflect on their own thinking processes. This experience suggested to all of us that we could, indeed present students with problems to solve and challenge them to become more aware of the kinds of intellectual processes they used: for example background knowledge.

Now, what does this episode illustrate? For me, it suggests that problems that will engage students in the kinds of thinking processes we deem appropriate can, indeed be located within the existing school curriculum.. I disagree with those persons who say problem solving is a more complex skill and should be relegated to the upper grades. Young children solve problems all the time. Piaget's research on object permanence shows that at eighteen months babies begin to inquire about the object that, once in front of them, is placed behind Mommy's back or under the rug. Kids are finding solutions to problems all the time, at home and in school -- as well as causing a few themselves. (Barell, p. 109)

Barell noted that these first graders had been asked to make a list of ways they had discovered to solve problems, and using background knowledge was one of the ways they had listed, among others. Another item on their list was "Understanding the problem." He says,

These children have learned, through practice in trying to figure out what to do in a complex situation, that one of the most important aspects is *understanding the problem.* Researchers on problem solving have come to the same conclusion: that understanding the nature of the problem, or attempting to make it more meaningful, is one of the keys to figuring out what to do...these children zeroed in on the vital core of problem solving and decision making. (Barell, p. 138_)

He continues,

We all know that younger students' thinking is qualitatively different from that of older ones, high school level. We did not find, however, that the lack of "formal operational" logic or abstract thinking in elementary school students was too much of a hindrance to their identifying their thinking processes. Even first graders can engage in problem solving and...respond critically to each others' solutions...can reflect upon their thinking and evaluate it by noticing when they are copying others' thinking and when their thinking is good because "I understood the problem." (Barell, p. 159)

Duckworth (1987) agrees with Barell that providing children opportunities for critical thinking is vital for their cognitive growth. She says,

When children are afforded the occasions to be intellectually creative -- by being offered matter to be concerned about intellectually and by having their ideas accepted -- then not only do they learn about the world, but as a happy side effect their general intellectual ability is stimulated as well. (Duckworth, p. 12-13)

She continues, "....The having of wonderful ideas, which I consider the essence of intellectual development, would depend...to an overwhelming extent on the occasions for having them." (Duckworth, p. 13)

Change in Emphasis Needed

In order for the students of today to become strong critical thinking citizens of tomorrow, emphasis in the classrooms must change from teaching to learning. John Dewey (1991) espoused this basic idea many years ago when he wrote

To pry into the familiar, the usual, the automatic, simply for the sake of making it conscious, simply for the sake of formulating it, is both an impertinent interference, and a source of boredom. To be forced to dwell consciously upon the accustomed is the essence of ennui; to pursue methods of instruction that have that tendency is deliberately to cultivate lack of interest. On the other hand, what has been said in criticism of merely routine forms of skill, what has been said about the importance of having a genuine problem, of introducing the novel, and of reaching a deposit of general meaning weighs on the other side of the scales. It is as fatal to good thinking to fail to make conscious the standing source of some error or failure as it is to pry needlessly into what works smoothly. (Dewey, p. 216)

That is, students must do the work and teachers must facilitate. Meaningful education takes time, is logically messy, requires opportunity for alternatives, and above all is political. Empowerment of students must begin in the schools at the earliest level such that students become aware of possibilities, will challenge what is presented as given, will demand to look at the evidence and examine reasons, and finally will take their places as full participants in a global society that must learn to treat its humblest citizens as it does the most powerful. It is the teacher's job, not to teach the students facts, if there is such a thing, but to facilitate their empowerment through the nature of the classroom environment and the problems and challenges we put before them. We must put to use the good critical thinking that students already use outside of school in the classroom so that students will examine the world around them critically in order to enhance the quality of life for the whole planet.

To make our classrooms micromodels of what is possible when all students are empowered in this way through critical thinking is to know the future. The answer, then, is yes. Yes, children can think critically during their early childhood years. Yes, they can think critically in early childhood classrooms in a school setting, and critical thinking can be made a vital part of their curriculum. That this should be done, is, in fact, critical.

BIBLIOGRAPHY

Adams, D. & Hamm, M., (1992, October). "Making Thinking Visible," Think:The magazine on critical & creative thinking, gr. K-8. San Antonio, TX: ECS Learning Systems.

Apple, M.W., & Christian-Smith, L. K., eds., (1991). The politics of the textbook. New York: Routledge.

Barell, J. (1991). Teaching for thoughtfulness: Classroom strategies to enhance intellectual development. New York: Longman.

Brooks, J., & Brooks, M., (1993). In search of understanding: The case for constructivist classrooms. Alexandria, VA: ASCD.

Dewey, J. (1991). How we think. Buffalo, NY: Prometheus Books.

Duckworth, E. (1987). "The having of wonderful ideas" and other essays on teaching and learning. New York: Teachers College Press, Columbia University.

Elias, M., "Everyday Decision Making and Problem Solving: An Instructional Imperative," Teaching thinking and problem solving: The newsletter for the thinking educator, Volume 14, Issue 1, January-February, 1992. Philadelphia, PA: Research for Better Schools.

Ennis, R. (1994, July). "Dispositions and abilities of idea critical thinkers," Critical thinking. Englewood Cliffs, NJ: Prentice Hall, forthcoming.

Gardner, H. (1983). Frames of mind: The theory of multiple intelligences, New York: Basic Books, Inc.

Gardner, H. (1993, April). "Interview," Think: A magazine on critical & creative thinking, gr. K-8. San Antonio, TX: ECS Learning Systems.

Giroux, Henry A., (1992). Border crossings: Cultural workers and the politics of education. New York, Routledge.

Giroux, Henry A., (1983). Theory and resistance in education: A pedagogy for the opposition. South Hadley, Mass., Bergen & Garvey.

Giroux, Henry A., (1981). Ideology, culture, and the process of schooling. Philadelphia, PA, Temple University Press.

Giroux, Henry A. & Purpel, David, eds., (1983). The hidden curriculum and moral education: Deception or discovery?. Berkeley, CA, McCutcheon.
Gitlin, A.D., (1990, November). "Educative research, voice and school change," Harvard Educational Review, 60(4), Boston: Harvard College.

Glass, G.V. & Hopkins, K.D., (1984). Statistical methods in education and psychology. Second edition. Boston: Allyn and Bacon.

Greene, M., (1991, November). "From thoughtfulness to critique: The teaching connection," Inquiry: Critical thinking across the disciplines. Upper Montclair, NJ: Institute for Critical Thinking, Montclair State College.

John-Steiner, V. (1985). Notebooks of the mind: Explorations of thinking. New York: Harper & Row.

Kohlberg, L. and Gilligan, C., (1972). "The adolescent as a philosopher: The discovery of the self in a postconventional world," Basic and contemporary issues in developmental psychology, Mussen, P., Conger, J. and Kagan, J., New York: Harper and Row.

Lather, P., (1986, August). "Research as Praxis," Harvard Educational Review, 56(3).

Lipman, M., (1988). "Critical Thinking: What Can It Be?" Institure for critical thinking resource publication series 1, No. 1. Upper Montclair, NJ: Montclair State College.

Lipman, M. (1988). Philosophy goes to school. Philadelphia: Temple University Press.

Mishler, E.G., (1990, November). "Validation in inquiry-guided research: The role of exemplars in narrative studies." Harvard Educational Review, 60(4).

Morgan, G., (1993, February). "You Say You Want a Revolution," Think: The magazine on critical & creative thinking, gr. K-8. San Antonio, TX: ECSS Learning Systems.

Paley, V. (1990). The boy who would be a helicopter. Cambridge: Harvard University Press.

Paul, Richard W., 1990. Critical thinking: What every person needs to survive in a rapidly changing world. A.J.A. Binker (Ed.). Rohbert Park, CA, Center for Critical Thinking and Moral Critique.

Peshkin, A., "In search of subjectivity -- one's own," Educational researcher, October, 1988.

Piaget, J.(1962). "The stages of the intellectual development of the child," Basic and contemporary issues in developmental psychology, Mussen, P., Conger, J., & Kagan, J., Harper & Row, New York.

Piaget, J.(1973). The child and reality: Problems of genetic psychology. (A. Rosin, trans.) New York: Grossman. (originally published 1972)

Piaget, J. (1985). The equilibration of cognitive structures. (T. Brown, trans.) Chicago: University of Chicago Press. (originally published 1975)

Quantz, R.A., & O'Connor, T.W., (1988, Winter). "Writing critical ethnography: Dialogue, multivoicedness, and carnival in cultural texts," Educational Theory, 38(1).

Reed, W. & Palumbo, D., (1992). " The Effect of BASIC Instruction on Problem Solving Skills over an Extended Period of Time," Journal of Educational Computing Research, Vol. 8(3) 311-325, 1992.

Ruggiero, V., (1990). Lessonpack for creative and critical thinking. Dunedin, FL: Mindbuilding.

Ruggiero, V., (1991). Teaching thinking. Dunedin, FL: Mindbuilding.

Swartz, R. & Parks, S., (1992, December). "Interview," Think: The magazine on critical & creative thinking, gr. K-8. San Antonio, TX: ECS Learning Systems.

Vygotsky, L. (1989) Thought and language. (A. Kozulin, Trans.) Cambridge, MA: The MIT Press. (Original work published 1934)

Weil, D. (1992, April). "Reasoning Readiness," Think:The magazine on critical & creative thinking, gr. K-8. San Antonio, TX: ECS Learning Systems.

Weinstein, M., (1991). "Critical Thinking and Education for Democracy," Institute for Critical Thinking Resource Publication, Series 4, No. 2. Upper Montclair, NJ: Institute for Critical Thinking, Montclair State College.

INDEX

MELLEN STUDIES IN EDUCATION

1. C. J. Schott, **Improving The Training and Evaluation of Teachers at the Secondary School Level: Educating the Educators in Pursuit of Excellence**

2. Manfred Prokop, **Learning Strategies For Second Language Users: An Analytical Appraisal with Case Studies**

3. Charles P. Nemeth, **A Status Report on Contemporary Criminal Justice Education: A Definition of the Discipline and an Assessment of Its Curricula, Faculty and Program Characteristics**

4. Stephen H. Barnes (ed.), **Points of View on American Higher Education: A Selection of Essays from** *The Chronicle of Higher Education* (Volume 1) **Professors and Scholarship**

5. Stephen H. Barnes (ed.), **Points of View on American Higher Education: A Selection of Essays from** *The Chronicle of Higher Education* (Volume 2) **Institutions and Issues**

6. Stephen H. Barnes (ed.), **Points of View on American Higher Education: A Selection of Essays from** *The Chronicle of Higher Education* (Volume 3) **Students and Standards**

7. Michael V. Belok and Thomas Metos, **The University President in Arizona 1945-1980: An Oral History**

8. Henry R. Weinstock and Charles J. Fazzaro, **Democratic Ideals and the Valuing of Knowledge In American Education: Two Contradictory Tendencies**

9. Arthur R. Crowell, Jr., **A Handbook For the Special Education Administrator: Organization and Procedures for Special Education**

10. J.J. Chambliss, **The Influence of Plato and Aristotle on John Dewey's Philosophy**